CONTENTS

INTRODUCTORY

PREFACE.

Those beginning the study of "French" at University are sometimes dismayed to find that the course consists as much of the literature of France as of its language. This is particularly true of students with little experience of literature. The concern of this book is wholly practical, not theoretical. Its function is not to say why so many British Universities emphasise the teaching of literature, but rather to help students to approach that literature through the exercise known as "literary commentary". To call it an introduction to literary study would be to overstate its pretensions; yet it is hoped that this little book will be of service to the student who is confronting literary studies - especially in a foreign language - for the first time.

Nor is the scope of the book limited to French. Although the examples are drawn from this area, the great majority of the analytical techniques and descriptive terms will be found to apply equally well to English, Spanish, German, Russian or any other literature.

WHAT IS COMMENTARY?

Different institutions, and even different individuals within a single institution, have varying ideas of what constitutes a "literary commentary". In order to help as many students as possible, we will in this book take a broad definition of the exercise as consisting of a detailed analysis, in English or French, of a short extract from a written text, usually a literary text. The purpose of the exercise is to bring out the particular qualities with which the author has consciously endowed his work, and the impact those qualities have on the reader.

It is as well to bear in mind from the very start that writing a commentary is quite unlike solving a mathematical problem. In maths, differing routes will lead to a single answer; in commentary, not only will the routes diverge, but there will be several answers, all of which may be equally correct. Because a good commentary is the product of informed individual response, there may be as many different answers as there are different individuals completing the exercise.

Literary Commentary, Critical Reading, Unseen Commentary, Close Reading, Literary Appreciation, Textual Commentary, "Explication de Texte", "Explication littéraire" ... Whatever the name, the exercise has a similar purpose. Reading is an art, and the commentary exercise is part of a training in that art. If successfully learnt, it will enable you to derive greater pleasure from reading, greater insight into the creative process, and greater awareness of the good and bad qualities of a book. It will enhance your appreciation and enjoyment of books.

The first step is to go beyond our everyday response to the masses of information that constantly bombard us in written or spoken form. Normally, we are concerned only with _what_ is said; in commentary, we look not only at the content but more particularly at _how_ something is said. And we look in great detail - the degree of analytical detail is what distinguishes a commentary from a general essay. A good author will choose his words carefully, so that they communicate the content in the fullest possible manner. The choice of expression is vital to the quality of the communication, as measured by its impact on the reader.

In commentary, the reader is _YOU_. The exercise is designed to develop in you the ability to analyse how a particular form of expression conveys to you, the reader, a particular impression. By analysing your response to a piece of writing, you will be developing the skills of literary criticism. The essence of the commentary exercise, then, is to assess and explain WHAT EFFECT THE AUTHOR HAS ACHIEVED, AND HOW HIS CHOICE OF EXPRESSION HAS ACHIEVED THAT EFFECT. If you bear that definition always in mind, you will not go far wrong.

CHOICES

All literary writing is a matter of conscious choices. When we write a letter to a friend, we tend to write spontaneously. We are thinking probably of what we want to tell them about, or what to ask them, but we do not pay much attention to the words we use to convey our message. Nor, when we receive a friendly letter, do we normally stop to ask ourselves whether it is well written or not: it is the content that counts.

If we are writing an essay for school or University, we are a bit more careful. We operate an automatic, unconscious selection process in avoiding certain expressions (slang or swear words, for instance). But we also operate at a _conscious_ level in choosing exactly those words which best express our opinions. We are aware that we will be judged partly on how well we have expressed ourselves, so we hesitate between alternative ways of wording an idea before selecting one of them.

Literary composition is an extension of this procedure of consciously choosing the expression to be used. The author operates a choice at every level:
what to write about
in what period the book will be set
who will be the narrator
what characters to introduce
what each character will be like
in what order to introduce them
at what stage to introduce them
what events will constitute the plot
in what order the events will occur
when each event will take place

In addition to these global considerations, the author, as he writes
every page, is making further conscious choices:
        what do I want to say next?
        how will this passage be structured?
        where do I want to begin a new paragraph?
        is this sentence too long or too short?
        what about some direct speech for variety's sake?
        which word is more appropriate in this context?
        should I emphasise this expression by changing the word order?
        would it be more dramatic to put it another way?
        is it in character for her to say this so bluntly?
        would a touch of humour be appropriate?
        is this sentence adequately balanced?
        can I find a better image?
        do the words sound right?

His choice, in almost every case, is a conscious one. Many authors
write and rewrite several times before they are satisfied enough with
what they have written to send it off to the publisher's. Even
instinctive writers check what they have written, applying conscious
judgment to each aspect of composition and expression, before any
reader sees their work. In literary commentary, we must always bear in
mind how the process of literary composition is made up of a series of
conscious choices, and we must make this the basis of our analysis.

When an author decides to use a particular word, a particular
structure, or a particular image, his choice is guided by the effect
he wants to have on the reader, whether it be to inform, to amuse, to
entertain, to instruct, to intrigue, to move or whatever else. In
writing a literary commentary, our central task is to analyse what
effect the author was trying to achieve, whether he has achieved it in
our case (intentions and achievements are not always the same thing),
and just how the conscious choices he made contributed to this effect.

YOUR READER

Whatever the nature of the extract you are working on, the
specific purpose of your commentary is to bring out for your reader
(in other words, whoever will be marking your commentary) the
particular qualities of that extract. Always bear in mind the
characteristics of the imaginary reader for whom you are writing:
he/she is intelligent, open-minded, and has a good command of French;
in the case of commentary on a set text, he/she will also be familiar
with the book as a whole. But you, the critic, are needed to analyse
for him/her exactly what the author is doing in the passage in
question. It is, of course, an artificial exercise, since your tutor
may or may not be intelligent, open-minded, with fluent French and an
intimate knowledge of the set texts. Moreover, he/she could probably
produce a better commentary than yours, at least initially. Commentary
is nonetheless a very valuable initiation into the brass tacks of
literary criticism.

THIS BOOK

Since a commentary analyses the response of individual A to a passage by individual B, the variety of possible commentaries is infinite, and this little book can only hope to offer some overall guidance: To do so, it is convenient to look in turn at different aspects of the exercise, and we will consider in successive sections: generalities; style; poetry; drama; commentary on a set text; historical perspective; and writing a commentary. After a summary and check-list, you will find two exercises.

Despite the distinction made here between unseen commentary - where you are writing about an extract you have never seen before from a book you know only vaguely if at all - and commentary on an extract from a set text, virtually all the remarks in earlier sections apply also to commentary on a set text.

EXAMPLES

Illustrations are not intended to be learnt by heart, but to be studied, so that you will recognise a similar technique when you encounter it elsewhere. The great majority are taken from _Pierre et Jean_ by Guy de Maupassant.

TERMINOLOGY

By the time you have finished reading this book, you should be equipped with a sufficient vocabulary to write commentaries. But, as you read, make sure that you really do understand any technical terms used in this book. We avoid unnecessary jargon wherever possible, but if, for example, you understood "criticism" to mean a _negative_ assessment rather than simply an assessment (which may equally be very favourable), then remember in future not to trust your intuition about what words mean, but to check their precise meaning in a dictionary. Terms traditionally used in literary commentary are printed in capitals.

COMPREHENSION

The next remark will seem unnecessary to you: before you can comment on a text, you need to understand it. Nonetheless, you would be surprised how many students tackle a text of which they have only an imperfect understanding.

For example, one girl responded to the phrase "le soleil se coucha" by suggesting it was personification, since the sun was going to bed. Worse misunderstandings are possible with phrases like "une toilette de l'ancien modèle, haute avec des tiroirs et des portes".

DICTIONARIES

Part of understanding a text is using a dictionary properly. If you look up a French word, you may find a variety of English equivalents opposite it; these must be taken together to give an approximation of the full sense of the French word. What you must not do is take just one of the proposed translations and assume that it is on its own a sufficient equivalent of the French word. An example of the dangers comes from a commentary on a passage containing the phrase "mettre la main dessus". One proffered translation was "to lay hands on", and one commentary duly explored the religious associations of the laying on of hands. More careful dictionary work would have shown that "mettre la main dessus" can only have the sense of "to lay hands on" when it means "to come across something", or "to pinch something"; it has no religious connotations at all. The moral is simple: if you have bought a pocket dictionary, give it to Oxfam. Always use a large dictionary, preferably two dictionaries together, one French-English and one (such as the Petit Robert) in French only, with examples of the kind of context in which the word is normally used.

As a practical illustration, take the word "flot", look it up in a pocket French-English dictionary, then in a more substantial bilingual dictionary, and finally in the Petit Robert. Meaning is not a matter of word-for-word equivalence, but of a central concept and a number of connotations and associations, many of which depend on context. Only with the help of the Petit Robert, which lists and defines near-synonyms of "flot" ("houle", "lame", "moutonnement", "onde", "vague", "vaguelette") will you grasp the precise image conjured up by "flot", and be able to appreciate the author's reasons for choosing it in preference to another word.

GRAMMAR TERMS

A further necessity is a sufficient command of grammatical terms. Literary criticism is awash with technical terms, most of which you can get by without. But even if you cannot distinguish a polysyndeton from an archaeopteryx, you must be familiar with the basic tools of the trade: you must be able to name the various constituent elements of written language. You must be able to recognise, for instance, an adverb, an adjective, a preposition, a conjunction, a superlative, a subordinate clause. In Glasgow University, a short book has been produced especially for students in your position: written by J.M.Y.Simpson, it is called Making Sense of Grammatical Terms, and is available in this same series.

INTEREST

Interest and "VRAISEMBLANCE" are two considerations that are so basic that you need not point them out - but do not forget them either. Firstly, any book should be interesting, otherwise no-one would read it. The usual means of arousing a reader's interest are

PLOT and CHARACTERS, both of which appeal to natural human curiosity, and the reader's interest is then sustained by a combination of suspense ("what happens next?") and of involvement with the characters.

VRAISEMBLANCE

In fiction, there is an unspoken convention between the author and his audience. The author will present his tale as if it might really have happened, and the audience, by what has been called a willing suspension of disbelief, accepts for the duration of the novel or play that its events really could have happened. Clearly, if the convention is to work, the piece of fiction needs to be, to some degree, "vraisemblable" or realistic, both physically in its setting and its events, and psychologically in the way the characters act. If these aspects are not convincing, the reader's interest may be lost, although in works of fantasy the definition of what is realistic can be stretched a bit. In recent years, television soap operas have shown how far suspension of disbelief can be pushed, both by introducing unlikely events, and by replacing established actors with new ones, while leaving characters and relationships unchanged.

Sometimes an author will deliberately break the illusion he has created, often by intruding personally into the story he is telling: such intervention undermines the reader's belief in what he is seeing or reading, an effect often exploited to draw attention to the tacit conventions of literature and drama.

In writing your commentary, it is up to you to show _how_ the author arouses and sustains your interest, and _how_ he establishes (or destroys) the "vraisemblance".

GENERALITIES

You are expected to comment on all the important stylistic details, but although it is these details which combine to create the overall nature of the extract, it is normal to begin a literary commentary with some introductory remarks on the nature of the passage as a whole. In what follows, these generalities are therefore covered first. After the generalities comes a listing of the kind of details which would require comment and which provide the main substance of your commentary.

NATURE OF THE PASSAGE: NARRATIVE AND DESCRIPTION

Distinguish NARRATIVE (the events of a story) from DESCRIPTION (which covers all those aspects of a scene which we perceive through the senses, or any representation in words of something we normally cannot perceive, such as a mood or a state of mind). Pure narrative is very rare, because to a simple list of events an author needs to add

descriptive detail if the reader is to be clear what is happening.
Notice the number of verbs in this example of a mainly narrative
passage:

> Et le docteur, impatienté, s'en alla, rentra dans la maison
> paternelle et se coucha. Pendant quelque temps, il entendit
> Jean qui marchait doucement dans la chambre voisine, puis il
> s'endormit après avoir bu deux verres d'eau.

Description can take many forms. It may be pure _physical_
description to serve as background. Background helps the reader to
visualise the scene in which the author will place the events of his
story. It is a matter of providing the scenery or the local colour -
the decor that is physically present on the stage or on television.
Here are three separate examples.

> Pierre se rendit sur la plage.
> De loin, elle avait l'air d'un long jardin plein de fleurs
> éclatantes. Sur la grande dune de sable jaune, depuis la
> jetée jusqu'aux Roches Noires, les ombrelles de toutes les
> 5 couleurs, les chapeaux de toutes les formes, les toilettes
> de toutes les nuances, par groupes devant les cabines, par
> lignes le long du flot ou dispersées çà et là, ressemblaient
> vraiment à des bouquets énormes dans une prairie démesurée.
> Et le bruit confus, proche et lointain des voix égrenées
> 10 dans l'air léger, les appels, les cris d'enfants qu'on
> baigne, les rires clairs des femmes faisaient une rumeur
> continue et douce, mêlée à la brise insensible et qu'on
> aspirait avec elle.

The colour and noise of the beach scene can be contrasted with a
picture of the autumn countryside:

> C'était l'époque des récoltes mûres. A côté des trèfles d'un
> vert sombre, et des betteraves d'un vert cru, les blés
> jaunes éclairaient la campagne d'une lueur dorée et blonde.
> Ils semblaient avoir bu la lumière du soleil tombée sur eux.
> 5 On commençait à moissonner par places, et dans les champs
> attaqués par les faux on voyait les hommes se balancer en
> promenant au ras du sol leur grande lame en forme d'aile.

Or with the cliffs where land and sea meet:

> Quand ils arrivèrent au bout du vallon, au bord de l'abîme,
> ils aperçurent un petit sentier qui descendait le long de la
> falaise, et sous eux, entre la mer et le pied de la
> montagne, à mi-côte à peu près, un surprenant chaos de
> 5 rochers énormes, écroulés, renversés, entassés les uns sur
> les autres dans une espèce de plaine herbeuse et mouvementée
> qui courait à perte de vue vers le sud, formée par les
> éboulements anciens. Sur cette longue bande de broussailles
> et de gazon secouée, eût-on dit, par des sursauts de volcan,
> 10 les rocs tombés semblaient les ruines d'une grande cité

disparue qui regardait autrefois l'Océan, dominée elle-même
par la muraille blanche et sans fin de la falaise.

An author may choose to describe a character in mainly visual
terms, with some hints as to his nature:

C'était un homme de soixante ans, portant en pointe sa barbe
blanche, avec des sourcils épais, tout blancs aussi. Il
n'était ni grand ni petit, avait l'air affable, les yeux
gris et doux, le geste modeste, l'aspect d'un brave être,
5   simple et tendre.

Compare this with a comically exaggerated portrait:

Il avait un gros ventre de boutiquier, rien qu'un ventre où
semblait réfugié le reste de son corps, un de ces ventres
mous d'hommes toujours assis qui n'ont plus ni cuisses, ni
poitrine, ni bras, ni cou, le fond de leur chaise ayant
5   tassé toute leur matière au même endroit.

In presenting his characters, a writer will want the reader to
respond to them, whether with sympathy, understanding, recognition,
distaste or objective judgment. And, in fact, description, in the
hands of a capable author, is very rarely neutral. A house can often
be a reflection of the people that live in it, while a description of
a village can bring out the circumstances that contributed to the
formation of a person's character. In the next example, physical
description evokes an atmosphere which echoes the mood of the walker:

Il sortit de bonne heure et se remit à rôder par les rues.
Elles étaient ensevelies sous le brouillard qui rendait
pesante, opaque et nauséabonde la nuit. On eût dit une fumée
pestilentielle abattue sur la terre. On la voyait passer sur
5   les becs de gaz qu'elle paraissait éteindre par moments. Les
pavés des rues devenaient glissants comme par les soirs de
verglas, et toutes les mauvaises odeurs semblaient sortir du
ventre des maisons, puanteurs des caves, des fosses, des
égouts, des cuisines pauvres, pour se mêler à l'affreuse
10   senteur de cette brume errante.

As you can see, there are many different kinds of physical
description which you should distinguish, not to mention the
reflective passages of what might be called psychological description,
where we learn of the state of mind of the characters.

The preface to Pierre et Jean is a different sort of writing
again: a logically developed argument, with illustrations. And of
course there are other kinds of passage still - some will be a
monologue or dialogue all in direct speech, others may be
philosophical discourse or advertising copy. Different elements, such
as narrative and description, are often combined within a single
passage.

POSITION OF NARRATOR

Any piece of writing is in either the first, the second or the third person:

FIRST PERSON: I did this, we did this
SECOND PERSON: You did this
THIRD PERSON: He did this, she did this, they did this, one does this, the Government did this, Jean did this, this has been done.

One of the most important choices an author has to make is the POINT OF VIEW from which the novel will be written. Will the narration be in the first, the second or the third person?

THIRD PERSON

By far the most common and straight-forward for novel-writing is the third person. It has been the traditional form in which to write a novel ever since the first European novels appeared in the sixteenth and seventeenth centuries. Why should the third person novel have become the standard?

The basic answer is that it can be the most realistic form of writing. Impartial history is written in the third person (Napoleon Bonaparte was born in Corsica in 1769 and completed his military education at Brienne) so that a fictional account written in the third person will appear to be impartial history, fact rather than fiction. The author is self-effacing to the point of invisibility. As you read a third person novel, the process of literary creation is far from your mind; it is as if there were no author, so that the facts presented have their own existence. For this reason, a third person narrative or description acquires an apparent objectivity.

Of course, this is just an illusion, but the reader's impression that he is reading a factual account can be so strong that he forgets that, in the real world, no one person could know all the events and private thoughts and conversations that appear in the book as if they had really happened. The OMNISCIENT NARRATOR has divine powers: he can see into the innermost, unspoken thoughts of all his creatures. As a result, the reader knows what they are all thinking in a way that is impossible in reality. In spite of this, with skilful writing, the illusion of realism can be maintained.

FIRST PERSON

The first person narrative is perhaps a more adaptable form. In the first place, it too can be said to have realism. While third-person narration has the realism of a history book, first-person presentation has the realism of the autobiography or the person-to-person conversation.

Because it resembles a conversation, writing in the first person can also seem more direct or intimate, as if the author is speaking to you face to face.

The authenticity of a first-person novel can go beyond that of a book employing the third person, by the very nature of its models. A history book is expected to be accurate and objective in every particular, whereas in an autobiography (and still more in a conversation), you expect the writer to have taken a certain liberty in the presentation of facts, to have interpreted them in his own way. You thereby learn not only of the facts, but also something of how the narrator feels about those facts - his subjective reality.

In narrative written from either a third- or a first-person viewpoint, you get a description of events and some insight into character ("he thought this" or "I thought this"). But in a first person narration you can get a deeper insight from what the author does not say, or from exactly how he says something. In Gide's L'Immoraliste, for example, the author makes the narrator and main character, Michel, betray himself by distorting the facts. The reader perceives the discrepancy between what really happened and the truth as Michel presents it, and is thus aware of the character's self-deception. And of course it is more convincing for the reader to spot this self-deception for himself (using the faculties we all apply every day in life) than simply to be told of it.

PERSONA

There is a further aspect of first-person writing you should be aware of, especially in dealing with poetry: a piece of literature is a work of craftsmanship rather than of self-revelation. The "I" of a first-person novel by Gide or a first-person poem by Baudelaire is not necessarily Gide or Baudelaire, but more likely a fictional "I", a PERSONA, adopted by the author for the purpose of the work. Be sure to distinguish between the real author and the fictional persona.

SECOND PERSON

Second-person narration is very rare, since it is very difficult to persuade a reader that the events described are actually happening to him or her. Nonetheless modern novels (e.g. Michel Butor's La Modification) have tried out the technique, and where a reader is eager to enter into a world of fantasy and illusion (as in adventure game books or computer games) the second-person presentation can be effective.

DIRECT SPEECH

It is very rare indeed to find a novel which consists entirely of narration and description, without passages of DIRECT SPEECH. Why do nearly all authors use it?

For one thing, people talking is closer to the reader's everyday reality than is sustained narrative. It also provides the variety which is necessary to sustain interest. A glance at a page of almost any novel will show the author using direct speech to achieve both of these objectives - variety and realism.

Direct speech is, in a sense, an amalgam of first- and third-person narration. It is presented as if it really happened, without any subjective interference on the author's part; but at the same time the speaker reveals something of his or her character, as we all do every time we open our mouths:

> Le vieux, attendri par l'ivresse, se mit à pleurer, et d'une
> voix bredouillante:
> "Un frère... vous savez... un de ceux qu'on ne retrouve
> plus... nous ne nous quittions pas... il dînait à la maison
> 5 tous les soirs... et il nous payait de petites fêtes au
> théâtre... je ne vous dis que ça... que ça... que ça... Un
> ami, un vrai... un vrai... n'est-ce pas, Louise?"

In plays, of course, the major means of presenting a person's character is by what he says in direct speech (the others being actions on stage, and what other characters say about the person).

Direct speech, especially if it breaks up a sustained piece of narrative or description, can have a dramatic effect. Here is an example of MONOLOGUE with dramatic impact:

> Plus il y songeait, plus il revivait le passé des dernières
> années, plus le docteur jugeait invraisemblable, incroyable
> cette différence établie entre eux.
> Et une souffrance aiguë, une inexprimable angoisse entrée
> 5 dans sa poitrine, faisait aller son coeur comme une loque
> agitée. Les ressorts en paraissaient brisés, et le sang y
> passait à flots, librement, en le secouant d'un ballottement
> tumultueux.
> Alors, à mi-voix, comme on parle dans les cauchemars, il
> 10 murmura: "Il faut savoir. Mon Dieu, il faut savoir."

DIALOGUE is frequently used, as in the following example, to dramatise a conflict between two characters or two points of view, so that their differences really stand out:

> Pierre tout à coup se leva:
> "Cristi! dit-il, la veuve avait l'air vannée ce soir, les
> excursions ne lui réussissent pas."
> Jean se sentit soulevé soudain par une de ces promptes et
> 5 furieuses colères de débonnaires blessés au coeur.
> Le souffle lui manquait tant son émotion était vive, et il
> balbutia:
> "Je te défends désormais de dire 'la veuve' quand tu

```
      parleras de Mme Rosémilly!"
10    Pierre se tourna vers lui, hautain:
      "Je crois que tu me donnes des ordres. Deviens-tu fou, par
      hasard?"
      Jean aussitôt s'était dressé:
      "Je ne deviens pas fou, mais j'en ai assez de tes manières
15    envers moi."
      Pierre ricana:
      "Envers toi? Est-ce que tu fais partie de Mme Rosémilly?"
      - Sache que Mme Rosémilly va devenir ma femme."
      L'autre rit plus fort:
20    "Ah! Ah! très bien. Je comprends maintenant pourquoi je ne
      devrai plus l'appeler 'la veuve'. Mais tu as pris une drôle
      de manière pour m'annoncer ton mariage.
      - Je te défends de plaisanter... tu entends... je te le
      défends!"
```

Literary dialogue is another of the many areas where conventions have grown up over the years, conventions which are tacitly accepted by author and reader alike. Dialogue in books is not realistic. It is much neater and more precise than the speech of even the most experienced public speaker. If you analyse carefully a recording of real speech, you will find it is full of hesitations, repetitions, false starts and interruptions. A transcription of genuine, spontaneous speech is often barely comprehensible. This is because the listener's brain filters out the sounds it doesn't need, and adds information derived from other clues such as the speaker's tone of voice, facial expression, body posture, gesture and eye contact. The result is satisfactory communication of meaning.

In writing, where all the visual and aural clues are absent, the author cannot reproduce the spontaneous jumble that is real speech, so he opts for an edited version of the message to be communicated, sometimes adding, as in the last line above, a hesitation or repetition to evoke the manner in which the words are delivered, sometimes hinting by punctuation (? or !) at the intonation or volume, sometimes using authorial description to evoke the features of speech which cannot be reproduced in writing: see, for example, in the last passage, the account of Jean's anger (ll.4-6), and the descriptive "il balbutia" (ll.6-7), "hautain" (l.10), and "Pierre ricana" (l.16). This convention had already proved acceptable to both writer and reader many centuries before the invention of tape recorders.

INDIRECT SPEECH

INDIRECT SPEECH ("style indirect" in French) is a rather less dramatic and often briefer way of introducing the realism of spoken communication. It is important to know how it is formed.

The direct speech

(1) "J'ai manqué à mon devoir."

would become in indirect speech

(2) Pierre pensa qu'il avait manqué à son devoir.

In other words, the quotation marks disappear, a phrase including a verb of šaying or thinking and a "que" is added, the perfect (or present or future) tense becomes pluperfect (or imperfect or conditional), and the first person pronoun and possessive adjective become third person.

Literary use is often made of what is known in French as "style indirect libre" (free indirect speech). This is simply the indirect speech stripped of its introductory clause ("Pierre pensa que"), and it gives us

(3) Il avait manqué à son devoir.

The important thing about "style indirect libre" is that there is no clear indication that it is a quotation. You can no longer tell, from statement (3), whether it is Pierre's opinion or whether the author is stating it as a fact. One effect of this blurring between opinion and fact is to suggest to the reader that the only reality is the one in the character's mind. Subjectivity and objectivity become confused. Fantasies acquire an air of reality from the descriptive, indicative tense. In an internal monologue ("monologue intérieur"), the reader can observe the character's mental processes as they occur.

There are many subtle uses of "style indirect libre". It may be exploited to introduce variety or concision, or its ambiguity may invite the reader to compare past and present, author's view and character's view. Implicit irony may expose a character's posturing or hypocrisy: Flaubert's Emma Bovary, for example, is by no means a fond mother, yet

Elle déclarait adorer les enfants; c'était sa consolation, sa joie, sa folie.

On the other hand, "style indirect libre" makes it possible for an author, without needing to reproduce exactly the words spoken, to retain, and integrate into his narrative, the vocabulary, the syntax and the inflexions of speech. Individual, recognisable speech patterns can be portrayed without interrupting the flow of the narrative. A character may be delineated, or parodied, or have his emotional state exposed, by the distinctive traits of his speech. His verbal peculiarities will stand out from the more formal register of the author's narrative. In this example the free indirect speech reproduces the eagerness and spontaneity of the declaration of love:

Le clerc se récria que les natures idéales étaient difficiles à comprendre. Lui, du premier coup d'oeil, il l'avait aimée.

You may well find it useful to look through a few pages of your set books, to see how easily you can distinguish the imperfect of the author's description from the imperfect of "style indirect libre", and decide exactly why the writer has chosen this means of presentation rather than impersonal narration or direct speech.

STRUCTURE

It is of the utmost importance to discern the structure of a passage, and not only because this will normally provide the structure of your commentary. The author has chosen the order in which he will recount things, just as he chose the point of view of the narrator. It is therefore up to you to see what the structure is and why he chose it: how does the organisation of the material contribute to what the author is saying?

It very often helps to divide the passage up into sections so that the overall structure is clearer (see below, p.48). It may also help to put yourself in the author's shoes: if your commentary is about page 139 of Le Père Goriot, imagine Balzac, having completed pages 1 to 138, faced with a blank piece of paper, and having to work out how he will arrange what comes next. But perhaps the best way to understand structure is to look at several examples, either by yourself or with your tutor/teacher.

A typical narrative extract progresses chronologically:

> Une fois marié, il vécut deux ou trois ans sur la fortune de
> sa femme, se levant tard, fumant dans de grandes pipes en
> porcelaine, ne rentrant le soir qu'après le spectacle et
> fréquentant les cafés. Le beau-père mourut et laissa peu˘de
> 5   chose; il en fut indigné, se lança dans la fabrique, y
> perdit quelque argent, puis se retira dans la campagne, où
> il voulut faire valoir.

If, in an extract of this kind, there is a FLASHBACK or a digression from the main narrative, it is there for a purpose. Some modern French authors, including Nouveaux Romanciers such as Robbe-Grillet, tease the reader by confusing the chronology of their books.

There is more to structure than mere chronology, however. There may be a balance between different sections, a build-up of tension, a CRESCENDO, a CLIMAX or ANTI-CLIMAX, or a significant turning-point. Look for example at the following two passages:

> (I) Il demeurait trop écrasé pour faire un mouvement ou pour
> avoir une volonté. Sa détresse devenait intolérable; et il
> sentait que, derrière la porte, sa mère était là qui avait
> tout entendu et qui attendait.
> 5   Que faisait-elle? Pas un mouvement, pas un frisson, pas un
> souffle, pas un soupir ne révélait la présence d'un être
> derrière cette planche. Se serait-elle sauvée? Mais par où?
> Si elle s'était sauvée... elle avait donc sauté de la

fenêtre dans la rue!
10 Un sursaut de frayeur le souleva, si prompt et si dominateur
qu'il enfonça plutôt qu'il n'ouvrit la porte et se jeta dans
sa chambre.
Elle semblait vide. Une seule bougie l'éclairait, posée sur
la commode.
15 Jean s'élança vers la fenêtre, elle était fermée, avec des
volets clos. Il se retourna, fouillant les coins noirs de
son regard anxieux, et il s'aperçut que les rideaux du lit
avaient été tirés. Il y courut et les ouvrit.

(II) Il avait dormi profondément quand le mouvement des matelots
le tira de son repos. Il faisait jour, le train de marée
arrivait au quai amenant les voyageurs de Paris.
Alors il erra sur le navire au milieu de ces gens affairés,
5 inquiets, cherchant leurs cabines, s'appelant, se
questionnant et se répondant au hasard, dans l'effarement du
voyage commencé. Après qu'il eut salué le capitaine et serré
la main de son compagnon le commissaire du bord, il entra
dans le salon où quelques Anglais sommeillaient déjà dans
10 les coins. La grande pièce aux murs de marbre blanc encadrés
de filets d'or prolongeait indéfiniment dans les glaces la
perspective de ses longues tables flanquées de deux lignes
illimitées de sièges tournants, en velours grenat. C'était
bien là le vaste hall flottant et cosmopolite où devaient
15 manger en commun les gens riches de tous les continents. Son
luxe opulent était celui des grands hôtels, des théâtres,
des lieux publics, le luxe imposant et banal qui satisfait
l'oeil des millionnaires. Le docteur allait passer dans la
partie du navire réservée à la seconde classe, quand il se
20 souvint qu'on avait embarqué la veille au soir un grand
troupeau d'émigrants, et il descendit dans l'entrepont. En y
pénétrant, il fut saisi par une odeur nauséabonde d'humanité
pauvre et malpropre, puanteur de chair nue plus écoeurante
que celle du poil ou de la laine des bêtes. Alors, dans une
25 sorte de souterrain obscur et bas, pareil aux galeries des
mines, Pierre aperçut des centaines d'hommes, de femmes et
d'enfants étendus sur des planches superposées ou grouillant
par tas sur le sol. Il ne distinguait point les visages mais
voyait vaguement cette foule sordide en haillons, cette
30 foule de misérables vaincus par la vie, épuisés, écrasés,
partant avec une femme maigre et des enfants exténués pour
une terre inconnue, où ils espéraient ne point mourir de
faim, peut-être.
Et songeant au travail passé, au travail perdu, aux efforts
35 stériles, à la lutte acharnée, reprise chaque jour en vain,
à l'énergie dépensée par ces gueux, qui allaient recommencer
encore, sans savoir où, cette existence d'abominable misère,
le docteur eut envie de leur crier: "Mais foutez-vous donc à
l'eau avec vos femelles et vos petits!" Et son coeur fut
40 tellement étreint par la pitié qu'il s'en alla, ne pouvant
supporter leur vue.

In the first passage, we begin with the anguished thoughts of Jean, and see them concretised (in "style indirect libre") into the fear that his mother may have killed herself (lines 1-9). Whereas imperfect tenses dominate this section, the second (ll.10-12) is marked by a series of past historics, the rapid actions reflecting Jean's desperation and increasing the tension. Two more imperfects set the scene (1.13), and further increase the suspense by delaying (for Jean and the reader) the discovery he will make. Finally, a series of verbs in the past historic (ll.15-18), each reflecting frantic activity, leads to the climax.

The structure of the central paragraph of the second passage is one of careful balance, where each element of the first scene - the individual, carefree first class passengers on "la Lorraine" and the luxury, spaciousness, richness and dazzling light of their accommodation - is contrasted with the appalling conditions of the steerage passengers.

A further element of structure is that of FOCUS, and you may well find it helpful, in determining the focus, to imagine the extract as a film. What would the camera be looking at? In the scene on board ship, we watch the doctor moving, then look with his eyes at the luxury contrasting with the squalor, then concentrate again on him and his reaction - an emotional response we are invited to share since we have experienced with him the horrific contrast between rich and poor. This could be seen as a circular structure, since it returns to its starting point.

Every passage will have its own structure: perhaps a paragraph of description to set the scene, then narrative to advance the action, then dialogue to bring a confrontation to its climax; or perhaps a series of logical steps in an argument. What you need to look out for are the movement in a passage, the changes in focus, the stages of development, the logical or chronological progression with any digressions, the relative balance or contrast between sections, and any particular stresses or omissions in narrative or description.

TONE

The tone of a passage is the overall mood it conveys. Is there an atmosphere of suspense, tension and fear? Or of calm and contentment? Is the tone purely factual? In an emotional passage, is the tone romantic? Anguished? Lyrical and poetic? Tragic? Satirical? Comic and light-hearted? Read a random page or two from your set texts and you should be able to say what the overall tone is.

Remember, though, that when you come to write a commentary, you will have to show how individual details come together to create the overall tone and the overall effect that the extract has on the reader. Bear in mind also that any introductory mention of overall tone should be brief, e.g. "In this humorous extract..."

REGISTER

The register is simply the level of language used in a passage. As in English, there are in French levels of language which run from emotional and slangy speech to over-precise, pedantic writing, with numerous shades in between. These registers in a foreign language will become easier to recognise as you become more familar with the language itself. Since, in commentary exercises, you normally meet only the formal register usually used for literary work, you need only comment on register if it really stands out: Maupassant's imitation of peasant speech, for example, or the Parisian "argot" of San Antonio, or the informality, in Camus' L'Etranger, of the perfect tense in narrative where the past historic used to be expected.

THEME

Many teachers will expect in the introduction a brief summary of the theme or topic or content of the commentary passage. Keep it short. For example, of Arthur Rimbaud's Le Dormeur du Val (see p.38), we could say that the portrayal of a dead young man in an idyllic, natural setting illustrates how wrong it is for man to defile, especially by war, the beautiful world he lives in. And of Maupassant's liner (see p.18) we could write that the juxtaposition of the conditions of life of the moneyed and of the impoverished classes points to a gross inequality, and not only on board ship. The content/topic of a commentary passage (the dead soldier by the stream, life on board a transatlantic liner) may often be usefully distinguished from its theme (the evil of war, social inequality): the first is a matter of fact, the second a matter of interpretation.

STYLE

IMAGERY.

"Image" is a word that has various different meanings according to its context. We are concerned here only with the literary meaning. This is very precise: it does not simply mean a picture; a literary image is a comparison. An IMAGE expresses one thing in terms of another.

What anyone who uses imagery is doing - and we all use imagery - is to draw attention to the points that the two sides of the comparison have in common. If one were to say, ungallantly, that a girl is built like a lumberjack with a face like the back of a bus, the two images would bring out, in the first case, massiveness, muscularity and lack of femininity, and, in the second case, plainness and unattractiveness.

The central notion (in this case the girl's build and face) is known as the TENOR of an image, the notion it is compared to (here "lumberjack" and "back of a bus") is called (in this case,

appropriately!) the VEHICLE. The force of an image derives from
finding similarities where they are least expected. The greater the
distance between the tenor and its vehicle, the greater will be the
effect on the reader of discovering unexpected parallels between
wholly dissimilar notions.

SIMILE AND METAPHOR

Distinguish between two sorts of image, the SIMILE (plural
"similes") and the METAPHOR.

A simile says that A is like B, i.e. states explicitly, by use of
an expression such as "like", "as", "as if", "it seemed", "such as",
that a comparison is being made: "Le visage du père Goriot ... s'était
allumé comme le soleil d'un beau jour."

A metaphor tends to be more striking, since it says that A is B,
or talks of A only in terms of B: "En prononçant le nom du père
Goriot, Eugène avait donné un coup de baguette magique."

Look for example at Maupassant's use of a simile in describing
the significance of psychology to the objective novel:

Ils cachent donc la psychologie au lieu de l'étaler, ils en
font la carcasse de l'oeuvre, comme l'ossature invisible est
la carcasse du corps humain. Le peintre qui fait notre
portrait ne montre pas notre squelette.

At first sight there seems little in common between psychology
and a skeleton. But what Maupassant is using the image to express is
that in such a novel psychology is as invisible but as all-important
as the bone-structure of the human body.

Another simile provides an instance of an EXTENDED IMAGE:

L'avant ouvrait la mer, comme le soc d'une charrue folle, et
l'onde soulevée, souple et blanche d'écume, s'arrondissait
et retombait, comme retombe, brune et lourde, la terre
labourée des champs.

The point in common here is the appearance of the water cut by
the ship's bow and the earth turned by the plough: visual images form
the largest category of all images. In English, "ploughing through the
water" is a DEAD METAPHOR, one so frequently used that people hardly
realise that it is an image at all. But in Maupassant's hands, it is
striking because of its precise suggestions of shape, movement and
texture.

As language progresses over the centuries, there is a tendency
for some images to lose their force completely: "charming", "enchanté"
and the French verb "manger" are examples of this. And as with all
figures of speech, overuse ("it's fantastic", "it's magic") leads to

loss of effectiveness. MIXED METAPHOR ("every time he opens his mouth he puts his foot in it") is avoided by most careful authors.

You should always try to assess how good an image is - a difficult and subjective task, but which should always involve at least two questions:

(1) how original is the comparison? - Maupassant's skeleton simile is the more striking for being unexpected;

(2) how closely does the comparison fit the context? - look at this example:

> J'ai marché tout droit jusqu'à ce que le soleil, devant moi, au bout du canal, faisant mine de rougeoyer dans la brume au moment de se coucher, m'apparût, aux trois quarts masqué par les nuages, comme le germe au bord d'un jaune d'oeuf.

The author here is describing sunset seen through a mist: most of it looks yellow through the clouds, but a little corner shows red. The visual aspect is conveyed by comparison with a egg-yolk, the colour and shape forming the essence of the comparison. But a mood is also evoked: the allusion to the bloody embryo that you get on egg-yolks is intended to arouse disgust in the reader, a feeling which corresponds closely to the feeling of disgust for life which is described in the surrounding paragraphs. The image is thus not only strikingly original, but also far more appropriate to the gloomy context than a prettier image could be.

A traditional use of imagery is to express the ABSTRACT through the CONCRETE; in other words to express in physical terms something that is normally perceived only intellectually and not through the senses. Maupassant's skeleton is one example; here are two more:

> Pierre était dans un de ces jours mornes où on regarde dans tous les coins de son âme, où on en secoue tous les plis.

> Mais il avait l'âme troublée par ce levain de jalousie qui fermentait en lui.

In each case, the abstract-concrete comparison tends to be striking because of the dissimilarity of the two sides of the image.

PERSONIFICATION

A particular form of metaphor is PERSONIFICATION. It can be effective and original to lend human characteristics to inanimate objects, such as the jetty in this extended image:

> Et on voyait d'autres navires, coiffés aussi de fumée, accourant de tous les points de l'horizon vers la jetée courte et blanche qui les avalait comme une bouche, l'un

après l'autre. Et les barques de pêche et les grands
5   voiliers aux mâtures légères glissant sur le ciel, traînées
par d'imperceptibles remorqueurs, arrivaient tous, vite ou
lentement, vers cet ogre dévorant, qui, de temps en temps,
semblait repu, et rejetait vers la pleine mer une autre
flotte de paquebots, de bricks, de goélettes, de trois-mâts
10   chargés de ramures emmêlées.

Other personifications appear more conventional:

Sur sa droite, au-dessus de Sainte-Adresse, les deux phares
électriques du cap de la Hève, semblables à deux cyclopes
monstrueux et jumeaux, jetaient sur la mer leurs longs et
puissants regards.

As with all commentary, the way to analyse imagery is to state
what effect is achieved and how it is achieved, beginning in this case
with the common link between the two sides of the comparison. Look for
the purpose of the image: is it simply visual, or is the author
seeking to evoke a particular mood or to highlight a particular
quality? Practise analysis of imagery on the following examples:

Et soudain (...) la sirène de la jetée hurla tout près de
lui. Sa clameur de monstre surnaturel, plus retentissante
que le tonnerre, rugissement sauvage et formidable fait pour
dominer les voix du vent et des vagues, se répandit dans les
5   ténèbres sur la mer invisible ensevelie sous les
brouillards.

Une heure plus tard il était étendu dans son petit lit marin,
étroit et long comme un cercueil.

OTHER FORMS OF COMPARISON

All imagery operates by ANALOGY, but the term is most often
encountered in analysis of arguments, where it refers to a reasoning
based on the fact that two different cases have parallel or similar
features. As a means of giving a concrete representation of a point of
view, analogy is a very useful tool, but arguing by analogy is often a
way of disguising a weak or illogical argument. Look at the rugby
analogy on page 34.

An ALLEGORY, in English, is an implied (i.e. not explicitly
stated) extended parallel, a narrative describing one subject under
the guise of another. A well-known example is Camus' La Peste, in
which the portrayal of life dominated by an outbreak of plague
parallels life under Nazi occupation and, on a more general level,
life confronted with Evil in its many forms, both natural and man-
made. The French term "allégorie" has a more restricted sense,
applying to the personification of abstract nouns (such as "Evil" in
the previous sentence, or "Souci" or "Jalousie"): it is common in
mediaeval romance and lyric poetry.

A MYTH is a story which may also be allegorical, since it portrays real qualities, attitudes or relationships through imaginary (often superhuman) characters and events. European authors, including Sartre, Camus, Giraudoux and many others, frequently use the classical myths of Greek and Rome as a vehicle for their own preoccupations and viewpoints.

By the use of SYMBOLISM (if we leave aside the Symbolist movement of nineteenth century France), an author can develop an allegorical meaning in addition to the literal one: windows, for example, in Flaubert's Madame Bovary, become a symbol of yearning for something beyond the confines of a dull life.

ALLUSIONS

There are many ways in which an author may introduce references to the literature of the past. An acknowledged quotation ("Selon l'avis de Montaigne...") can lend authority to a point of view, while a recognisable but unattributed allusion can both flatter the reader and set up echoes in his mind. PASTICHE is imitation without mockery, while PARODY is a recognisable imitation of a work or style which brings out its latent potential for ridicule. Allusions to real places or events can enhance the realism of a fictional tale - a trick parodied in Voltaire's Candide.

SENTENCE STRUCTURE

In a good piece of writing, the words used and the order in which they are used combine, so that the arrangement of the words reinforces their sense, or adds another dimension to the communication. There are various ways in which this can be done.

COMPLEXITY, SIMPLICITY AND LENGTH

Look at this paragraph:

L'habileté de son plan ne consistera donc point dans l'émotion ou dans le charme, dans un début attachant ou dans une catastrophe émouvante, mais dans le groupement adroit de petits faits constants d'où se dégagera le sens définitif de
5 l'oeuvre. S'il fait tenir dans trois cents pages dix ans d'une vie pour montrer quelle a été, au milieu de tous les êtres qui l'ont entourée, sa signification particulière et bien caractéristique, il devra savoir éliminer, parmi les menus événements innombrables et quotidiens, tous ceux qui
10 lui sont inutiles, et mettre en lumière, d'une façon spéciale, tous ceux qui seraient demeurés inaperçus pour les observateurs peu clairvoyants et qui donnent au livre sa portée, sa valeur d'ensemble.

Maupassant's argument is complex, and so it is best expressed in these two long, complex sentences, with several dependent clauses, and with the parallel or contrasting elements carefully balanced. Short, simple sentences, on the other hand, because they are easily and rapidly assimilated by the reader, can have different effects. Advertising always uses short sentences, or even half-sentences, so that the reader is sure to absorb the message in small doses, without any effort from the intelligence. Short sentences facilitate rapid comprehension, and, because they are absorbed quickly, can also contribute to an atmosphere of drama, tension, suspense or rapid action.

As with all literary devices, restraint heightens the effect: a short sentence is more striking if it stands out from the other sentences around it. Following a number of longer sentences, it can be dramatic, and this is especially true in the stressed position at the end of a paragraph:

Et tout seul en errant par la nuit, il allait faire, dans ses souvenirs, dans sa raison, l'enquête minutieuse d'où résulterait l'éclatante vérité. Après cela ce serait fini, il n'y penserait plus, plus jamais. Il irait dormir.

Here the shortness of the final sentence emphasises its finality: sleep will put an end to all his torment.

RHYTHM

In general, a series of short words speeds up a narration, while long words slow it down. In order to give an impression of rapid, breathless action, an author will often employ ellipsis, i.e. omit parts of speech, especially personal and relative pronouns and conjunctions:

Dominant sa peur, elle se leva, traversa sa chambre sur la pointe des pieds, ouvrit sa porte avec précaution.

This author succeeds in increasing the excitement by leaving out inessential words ("puis", "et", "elle") to accelerate the rhythm.

The structure of a sentence can also provide harmony, symmetry, emphasis or memorability through a balance of either two or three parallel expressions. Such rhythm is known as binary (see, in the Gide extract which concludes this section on rhythm, the phrases involving "feuilles") or, where there are three parallel elements, ternary (or triple or trinary) rhythm:

Et je me laissais rêver à telles terres où toutes forces fussent si bien réglées, toutes dépenses si compensées, tous échanges si stricts...

Triple rhythm is particularly effective (Faith, Hope and Charity; Liberté, Egalité, Fraternité; Snap, Crackle and Pop; Beanz meanz Heinz) and very frequent, especially in oratory.

Rhythm can also make a piece of prose almost into poetry, creating balance and harmony by careful choice of the number and stresses of the syllables. See how Gide achieves a poetic rhythm by careful choice and arrangement of words: four 8-syllable phrases at the beginning and end, with a more wistful rhythm in the middle.

- Ou d'aller encore une fois, ô forêt pleine de mystère, jusqu'à ce lieu que je connais, où, dans une eau morte et brunie, trempent et s'amollissent encore les feuilles des ans passés, les feuilles des printemps adorables. C'est là que se reposent le mieux mes résolutions inutiles, et que se réduit à la fin, à peu de chose, ma pensée.

RHETORICAL DEVICES

Both imagery and sentence structure are part of the discipline of rhetoric - the art of speaking and writing effectively, which was for centuries a central element of European education. It is worth noting other rhetorical devices if you come across them in a commentary passage. Exclamations are very common:

Illusion du beau qui est une convention humaine! Illusion du laid qui est une opinion changeante! Illusion du vrai jamais immuable! Illusion de l'ignoble qui attire tant d'êtres!

A similar emphasis is achieved by the rhetorical question:

Si Don Quichotte est un roman, Le Rouge et le Noir en est-il un autre? Si Monte-Cristo est un roman, L'Assommoir en est-il un? Peut-on établir une comparaison entre Les Affinités électives de Goethe , Les Trois Mousquetaires de Dumas, Madame Bovary de Flaubert, M. de Camors de M. O. Feuillet et Germinal de M. Zola? Laquelle de ces oeuvres est un roman? Quelles sont ces fameuses règles? D'où viennent-elles? Qui les a établies? En vertu de quel principe, de quel autorité et de quels raisonnements?

There are a great number of figures of speech which were included in a classical education in rhetoric, some of the commonest being: Anacolutha: change of grammatical construction in mid-sentence:
O ciel! plus j'examine, et plus je le regarde,
C'est lui!
Anaphora: several lines of verse opening in the same way:
Puis Cydre où fut Crésus, le maître universel,
Puis Anane, et l'étang d'où l'on tire le sel;
Puis on vit Canos, mont plus affreux que l'Erèbe ...
Antiphrasis: irony, meaning the opposite of what is said, e.g. "Quel ordre, quelle propreté!" in the face of dirt and chaos.

Apostrophe: direct address to the reader or another:
Dieux, vous êtes cruels, jaloux de notre temps!
Chiasmus: structure in which elements are repeated in reverse order:
Un roi chantait en bas, en haut mourait un Dieu.
Hyperbole: emphasis by overstatement: "Le 1er mai est une fête
nationale. Tous les Français, toutes les Françaises l'acclament
de tout leur coeur." (De Gaulle)
Litotes: understatement, e.g. "pas mal" for very good.
Metonymy: replacing one word by a related term, e.g. "le trône" (for
monarchy), "les fers" (for imprisonment).
Oxymoron: self-contradictory expression, e.g. "l'obscure clarté", "de
hideuses délices".
Periphrasis: allusion to a person or thing by his/its qualities, not
by name, e.g. "les neuf soeurs" for the Muses.
Synecdoche: part for the whole or whole for the part, e.g. "deux
voiles" for two ships.
Zeugma: Linking two or more terms from different categories (e.g. 1
abstract and 1 concrete noun) to a single verb, adjective or
preposition. A fat man, for example, "se sentait teriblement
isolé, dans sa graisse et dans sa laideur".

For French translations of these terms and others, with
definitions and examples, see J.D. Biard's cheap and useful Lexique
pour l'explication de texte (University of Exeter, 1980).

WORD ORDER

Many of these figures of speech are concerned with drawing
attention to one element of a phrase. Emphasis can also be created by
word order: displacing a word from its usual position in a sentence
draws attention to it. An adverb normally follows the verb, so when it
comes before it:

Et Gervaise lentement promenait son regard...

it is stressed. Likewise, an adjective is emphasised when it precedes
a noun it would usually follow:

... cet invincible repos ... l'affreuse lumière du désastre
... la misérable enfant ... l'étroite église ...

Other positions of emphasis in French are at the beginning of a
sentence:

Enfermée, emprisonnée dans la boutique à côté d'un mari
vulgaire et parlant toujours commerce, elle avait rêvé de
clairs de lune...

Jamais, avant le retour de ses fils, le père Roland ne
l'avait invitée...

and at the end of a sentence:

Non, non, Jean ne lui ressemblait en rien.

See also the liner passage, p.18, end of paragraph 2.

Most sentences, in French as in English, begin with a subject
then a verb; as a result, if either or both are held back, the reader
unconsciously looks for a subject and verb, and his attention is kept
in suspense until he finds them:

<blockquote>
Cette pièce à meubles de bambou, à magots, à potiches, à
soieries pailletées d'or, à stores transparents où des
perles de verre semblaient des gouttes d'eau, à éventails
cloués au mur pour maintenir les étoffes, avec ses écrans,
5   ses sabres, ses masques, ses grues faites en plumes
véritables, tous ses menus bibelots de porcelaine, de bois,
de papier, d'ivoire, de nacre et de bronze, avait l'aspect
prétentieux et maniéré que donnent les mains inhabiles et
les yeux ignorants aux choses qui exigent le plus de tact,
10 de goût et d'éducation artiste.
</blockquote>

Not only does this maintain the reader's interest, it may also give
emphasis to the subject and/or verb (in this instance the verb
introduces a judgment on the room) when they do occur.

VOCABULARY

Apart from their sense, the nature of individual words
contributes a good deal to the overall impact of a passage. A whole
range of terms can be used to define the predominant nature of the
vocabulary of an extract; make sure you understand these: precise,
vague, ambiguous, enigmatic, banal, evocative, rich in association,
figurative, sensual, emotive, exotic, erotic, religious, mystical,
hyperbolic, understated, superlative, negative, ironic, idiomatic,
abstract, concrete, onomatopoeic, technical, archaic, pedantic,
didactic, humorous, comic, incongruous; pun, cliché, neologism,
circumlocution.

The relative weighting of different parts of speech will affect
the impact of a passage: a large number of conjunctions would suggest
a sophisticated argument, while nouns could lend a solid quality - or
an abstract one. There are two classes of words above all that you
should never let pass without examination: verbs and adjectives.

VERBS

As you should know, in formal writing in the past in French, the
past historic is used for narrative, and the imperfect for
description. This is the standard usage, and when the usage is
standard you need make no comment on the tenses of the verbs. But

where there is a departure from standard usage, point it out and ask
yourself why. Here, for instance,

> Comme on allait procéder à la troisième course, Candide,
> n'en pouvant plus, demanda en grâce qu'on voulût bien avoir
> la bonté de lui casser la tête: il obtint cette faveur; on
> lui bande les yeux; on le fait mettre à genoux.

we have (as well as irony) two examples of the HISTORIC PRESENT:
"bande" and "fait". This is a device, fairly conventional in formal
French writing, which makes events that happened in the past seem
closer to the present.

In Camus' L'Etranger, the past tense used for narrative is the
perfect. This is the informal past tense you use in speech, and when
used in a novel in place of the expected past historic, it again
brings the events related closer to the reader, as well as implying
that the first person narrator, Meursault, is by no means a skilled
writer. An imperfect in past narration can increase suspense by
slowing the action so that the reader perceives it with the
protagonist, as uncompleted. Consider this extract from Madame Bovary:

> Elle ouvrit les narines à plusieurs reprises, fortement,
> pour aspirer la fraîcheur des lierres autour des chapiteaux.
> Elle retira ses gants, elle s'essuya les mains; puis, avec
> son mouchoir, elle s'éventait la figure, tandis qu'à travers
> le battement de ses tempes elle entendait la rumeur de la
> foule et la voix du Conseiller qui psalmodiait ses phrases.

Use of other tenses in narrative is unusual, though the future
can suggest probability:

> Il sera passé à côté d'elle, juste à côté d'elle, sans la
> voir.

Apart from the tenses of verbs, look at their frequency. A
succession of active verbs or present participles indicates a lot of
movement or excitement (see lines 5-6 of the liner passage on p.18).
On the other hand, a series of passive verbs or repetition of "être"
or "rester" can suggest that a character is unwilling or unable to
take any action (look at the opening paragraph of the second passage
on p.17).

ADJECTIVES

A lack of adjectives is unusual - it can make a passage appear
stark and colourless. Where you have adjectives, see what function
they fulfil: do they appeal to the intellect, to the emotions, or to
the senses? Make the same distinction as between background and
atmospheric descriptions, but analyse this time in more detail. To
which senses is the author appealing - sight, hearing, smell, touch?
Is there a dominant colour, and is this just background or does it

correspond to a mood. Analyse, for instance, the colours in this passage:

> Sur la mer plate, tendue comme une étoffe bleue, immense, luisante, aux reflets d'or et de feu, s'élevait là-bas, dans la direction indiquée, un nuage noirâtre sur le ciel rose.

A distinctive adjective ("un arbre puissant") will always be more effective than a banal one ("un grand arbre").

It is important to practise analysing vocabulary. How, for instance, would you describe the lexis in the first example of personification (pp.22-3 above)? Or in this passage from Balzac:

> Cecy est ung livre de haulte digestion, plein de deduicts de grant goust, espicez pour ces goutteux trez-illustres et beuveurs trez-prétieux auxquels s'adressoyt nostre digne compatriote, éternel honneur de Touraine, François Rabelays.

In the first case you should have mentioned the different sea-going craft listed, in the second the deliberate archaism. Now write fuller notes on the lexis used in the descriptions of the beach (p.10), the cliffs (pp.10-11), and the fog (p.11). Once your notes are complete, compare them with what follows.

The beach.
Features of landscape - "dune de sable" in line 3, "jetée", "Roches" 4 -
and man-made objects - "ombrelles" 4, "chapeaux", "toilettes" 5 -
are colourful - "éclatantes", "jaune" 3, "Noires" 4, "toutes les couleurs" 4-5, "toutes les nuances" 6 -
especially natural colours - "jardin", "fleurs" 2, "bouquets", "prairie" 8.
Large numbers over a large area - "grande" 3, "depuis... jusqu'à" 3-4, "groupes" 6, "lignes", "le long", "dispersées çà et là" 7, "énormes", "démesurée" 8.
Noise, again characterised by numbers, variety and extent - "bruit confus", "proche", "lointain", "voix égrenées" 9, "appels", "cris d'enfants" 10, "rires" 11, "rumeur continue" 11-12.
Gentleness, lightness of air - "air léger" 10, "rires clairs" 11, "rumeur... douce" 11-12, "brise insensible" 12, "aspirait" 13.

The Cliffs.
Geographical features of considerable size - "vallon", "abîme" 1, "falaise", "mer" 3, "montagne" 4, "rochers énormes" 5, "volcan" 9, "grande" 10, "Océan" 11, "muraille... sans fin", "falaise" 12;
Passive victims of violent, destructive force in the past - "chaos" 4, "écroulés", "renversés", "entassés" 5, "mouvementée" 6, "éboulements anciens" 8, "secouée", "sursauts" 9, "tombés", "ruines" 10, "disparue", "autrefois", "dominée" 11.

The Fog.
Oppression - "ensevelies" 2, "pesante" 3, "abattue" 4, "toutes" 7.
Foul smell - "nauséabonde" 3, "pestilentielle" 4, "mauvaises odeurs"
7, "ventre", "puanteurs", "caves", "fosses" 8, "égouts",
"cuisines pauvres" 9, "affreuse senteur" 9-10.
Thickness - "opaque", "fumée" 3, obscures gas lights 4-5, "brume" 10.
Subjective impression (similes) - "On eût dit" 3, "paraissait" 5,
"comme" 6, "semblaient" 7.

COMBINATIONS OF VOCABULARY

An unusual combination of words can often be more expressive than
a more conventional and apparently more appropriate one. Eluard's
famous line

La terre est bleue comme une orange

seems nonsense at first, but in fact evokes a lot of ideas - blue sky,
roundness, fruitfulness, sunshine - that a more conventional simile
could not.

Juxtaposition (placing side by side) of words which do not
usually go together can be used for different effects, disturbing or
amusing, but always striking, so worthy of comment.

Also worth mentioning is any effect of contrast. This works in
literature as it does with vision: a white object on a white table
does not show up, but put it on a black table and you draw attention
to both the whiteness of the object and the blackness of the table.
Look at these passages to see how antithesis (contrast) is variously
used (I) to balance two paragraphs (note the details of structure),
(II) to oppose two sets of adjectives, and (III) to isolate Pierre.

(I)   Le romancier qui transforme la vérité constante, brutale et
       déplaisante, pour en tirer une aventure exceptionnelle et
       séduisante, doit, sans souci exagéré de la vraisemblance,
       manipuler les événements à son gré, les préparer et les
5   arranger pour plaire au lecteur, l'émouvoir ou l'attendrir.
       Le plan de son roman n'est qu'une série de combinaisons
       ingénieuses conduisant avec adresse au dénouement, Les
       incidents sont disposés et gradués vers le point culminant
       et l'effet de la fin, qui est un événement capital et
10   décisif, satisfaisant toutes les curiosités éveillées au
       début, metant une barrière à l'intérêt, et terminant si
       complètement l'histoire racontée qu'on ne désire plus savoir
       ce que deviendront, le lendemain, les personnages les plus
       attachants.
15   Le romancier, au contraire, qui prétend nous donner une
       image exacte de la vie, doit éviter avec soin tout
       enchaînement d'événements qui paraîtrait exceptionnel. Son
       but n'est point de nous raconter une histoire, de nous
       amuser ou de nous attendrir, mais de nous forcer à penser, à

20 comprendre le sens profond et caché des événements. A force
d'avoir vu et médité il regarde l'univers, les choses, les
faits et les hommes d'une certaine façon qui lui est propre
et qui résulte de l'ensemble de ses observations réfléchies.
C'est cette vision personnelle du monde qu'il cherche à nous
25 communiquer en la reproduisant dans un livre.

(II) Quel que soit le génie d'un homme faible, doux, sans
passions, aimant uniquement la science et le travail, jamais
il ne pourra se transporter assez complètement dans l'âme et
dans le corps d'un gaillard exubérant, sensuel, violent,
5 soulevé par tous les désirs et même par tous les vices, pour
comprendre et indiquer les impulsions et les sensations les
plus intimes de cet être si différent.

(III) Après le potage on offrit du madère; et tout le monde déjà
parlait en même temps. Beausire racontait un dîner qu'il
avait fait à Saint-Domingue à la table d'un général nègre.
Le père Roland l'écoutait, tout en cherchant à glisser entre
5 les phrases le récit d'un autre repas donné par un de ses
amis, à Meudon, et dont chaque convive avait été quinze
jours malade. Mme Rosémilly, Jean et sa mère faisaient un
projet d'excursion et de déjeuner à Saint-Jouin, dont ils se
promettaient déjà un plaisir infini; et Pierre regrettait de
10 ne pas avoir dîné seul, dans une gargote au bord de la mer,
pour éviter tout ce bruit, ces rires et cette joie qui
l'énervaient.

A PARADOX is a kind of intellectual contrast, in which two
apparently irreconcileable concepts are presented in combination, as
when Camus, having described the eternal punishment suffered in Hades
by Sisyphus, asserts that "il faut imaginer Sisyphe heureux".

One final aspect of the arrangement of words is the particular
emphasis that comes from REPETITION of similar terms. This can take
the form of a GRADATION:

Vous sentez vos muscles et vos tendons se dessiner non
seulement dans vos phalanges, dans votre paume, votre
poignet et votre bras, mais dans votre épaule aussi, dans
toute la moitié du dos et dans vos vertèbres depuis votre
5 cou jusqu'aux reins.

or of an ENUMERATION or list, where the impression is one of
completeness and universality:

Donc, après les écoles littéraires qui ont voulu nous donner
une vision déformée, surhumaine, poétique, attendrissante,
charmante ou superbe de la vie, est venue une école réaliste
ou naturaliste qui a prétendu nous montrer la vérité, rien
5 que la vérité et toute la vérité.

Or you can get an ACCUMULATION of terms which all point to the same

fact, as in the opening of the third paragraph of the liner passage
(p.18).

A NOTE ON. PUNCTUATION

You will not often need to comment on punctuation as such, but
you must be aware of its function. Basically, punctuation in written
language is a codified attempt to convey everything that, in spoken
language, is conveyed by non-verbal means, in other words by gestures,
pauses and intonation rather than by words. In speech, for instance,
you can tell the difference between "Vous êtes prêt?" (rising
intonation in a question) and "Vous êtes prêt." (falling intonation in
a statement). When written down, the punctuation marks are needed to
make the meaning clear.

Punctuation has, however, evolved conventions of its own. In a
list, for example, all items except the last two are separated by
commas. Commas also distinguish between a restrictive and a non-
restrictive relative clause, or between sentences like these:

The tutor thinks his student is a buffoon.

The tutor, thinks his student, is a buffoon.

As far as commentary is concerned, simply remember that an exclamation
mark indicates a more forceful intonation than would a full-stop, and
that a comma, semi-colon and full-stop indicate successively longer
pauses: this is particularly important in poetry where a long pause in
the middle of a line marks a very special effect.

The "points de suspension" or "trois points", far more common in
French than in English, indicate that a sentence is not complete. They
suggest either a break in speech, or an interruption, or simply that
the thought tails off (see examples in direct speech on pp.14-15
above).

POETRY

The differences between poetry and prose appear to be obvious,
but it may be useful to review them :

1 Poems tend to be shorter than prose works, so the effects must
be more concise, more concentrated: the choice of each individual
word is even more crucial.

2 Poetry is generally intended to be read out loud, so that the
sounds of a poem are immeasurably more important than in prose.

3 Most poetry has a formal aspect to be respected: a system of
rhyme, length of line and length of stanza.

In rugby, a player may kick for touch from behind his own 22-metre line, and the line-out is taken at the point where the ball went out of play. If, however, the player is in front of his own 22-metre line, and if the ball does not bounce before going out of play, the line-out takes place not where the ball went into touch, but at a point on the touchline level with the spot from which the player kicked.

All this sounds complicated, arbitrary, and totally unnecessary. Yet the practical result of these constraints is a more entertaining game of rugby. And, in the same way, the restrictions enumerated in (3), which at first seem to be merely artificial conventions which stifle creativity, can be exploited by a skilful poet to enhance the impact and expressiveness of his poetry.

In many senses the poet has greater resources available to him than has the prose writer. Both use the SENSE of words and the STRUCTURE which arises from arranging them in a particular order, but the poet can also exploit the SOUND of words, the RHYME of his lines, and the RHYTHM of his sentences to reinforce the sense of the words. The result is a fuller, richer communication in a more concentrated form.

I will be dealing with these resources under separate headings, but you must remember that they are invariably used in conjunction, each contributing to the same overall effect.

PREPARATION

Before attempting a literary assessment of any poem, you must read it out loud. Remember too that, while noting down your first impressions is important for any commentary, it is particularly so with poetry. First impressions will include not only the sounds of the poem, but also its title. The title of Rimbaud's Le Dormeur du val, for example, evokes a natural scene of tranquillity and security which will be described in the opening lines of the sonnet.

SENSE AND STRUCTURE

For the sense of words, their connotations and associations, and the overall structure of a poem, the same criteria apply as in prose (although, of course, when writing a commentary on a poem, you can grasp the entire structure of the whole piece, which is not the case with an extract from a novel). The grammatical structure operates in the same way, too, although "poetic licence" may sometimes permit the use of constructions, especially inverted word order, which would be frowned on in prose. This section therefore concentrates on the resources which belong more specifically to the domain of poetry: RHYTHM, RHYME and SOUND.

RHYTHM

The structure of a poem in French depends not only on grammatical structure, but also, perhaps even more so, on the rhythmic patterns. And here, we notice a very big difference from English poetry - read out loud these two lines by Byron:

The Assyrian came down like the wolf on the fold
And his cohorts were gleaming in purple and gold;

You will have heard yourself stressing certain syllables, and leaving others unstressed, as we all do in everyday speech:

The As_syr_ian came _down_ like a _wolf_ on the _fold_
And his _co_horts were _glea_ming in _pur_ple and _gold_.

English verse is characterised by a regular pattern of stressed syllables, in other words a regular rhythm. It does not really matter how many unstressed syllables are squeezed in between the stressed ones, provided that the rhythm (of stressed syllables) remains the same.

But French is a language which, in everyday use, does not have a large number of heavily stressed syllables, and its poetic conventions have evolved quite differently, so that the formal structure of the poem (the metre) is determined by the number of syllables in the line, while the stress can move about, allowing a great deal of expressiveness through rhythmic variation.

This is an important point to remember: the syllable count gives you the formal aspect of the poem, but its sound, and consequently its expressiveness and its musicality, depends on the rhythm of stressed syllables.

SYLLABLE COUNT

You must become familiar with the way syllables are counted and how French poetry sounds when read aloud. Although the conventions covering every eventuality can become complex, the basic rules are very simple. In most cases, the syllables sound as they do in spoken French. The one big exception is the mute "-e" at the end of a word. (Mute "-e" is the normally silent last syllable of words like être, rou_ge_, vit_e_, vill_es_, or ils vienn_ent_.) The rule for poetry is as follows:

IN THE BODY OF THE VERSE, MUTE "-E" DOES COUNT AS A SYLLABLE IF IT IS FOLLOWED BY "-S" OR "-NT", OR IF THE NEXT WORD BEGINS WITH A CONSONANT OR AN ASPIRATE "H". IT DOES NOT COUNT AS A SYLLABLE IF FOLLOWED BY A VOWEL OR A SILENT "H", OR AT THE END OF A LINE.

The mute "-e" is audible but unstressed, pronounced like the first vowel in "petit" or the vowel in the second word of "rue de la Paix".

Some examples (taken from Voltaire) should make the rule clear:

1   Je vois que mes malheurs excit<u>ent</u> vos refus.
     1   2   3   4   5   6   7 8 9   10 11 12
2   Par<u>t</u>ez; de votr<u>e</u> sort vous êt<u>es</u> encor maîtr<u>e</u>;
     1   2   3   4   5   6   7   8 9   10 11   12
3   O Corinth<u>e</u>! ô Phocid<u>e</u>! exécrabl<u>e</u> hyménée!
     1 2 3   4   5   6   7 8   9   10 11 12

If we disregard the cases where the letter "e" will always count as a syllable ("Je", "que", "refus", etc.) and look at those underlined, we see that the last syllable of "excitent", "votre" and "êtes" is pronounced because it is followed by "-nt", a consonant, and "-s" respectively, and that the mute "-e" of "Corinthe", "Phocide" and "exécrable" is elided because of a following vowel or silent "h". That of "maître" does not count, since it comes at the end of a line.

As for the aspirate "h", the effect is the same as in prose: "le hibou" would count for three syllables, but French poets normally prefer to avoid the HIATUS of successive sounded vowels, especially if they have the same sound ("Dalida alla à Arles"; "élevé et éduqué").

Diphthongs usually count as a single syllable, though by tradition some ("bien", the ending "-tion", etc.) can count as one or two syllables, as the poet wishes.

PRACTICE

Cover the facing page, then count the syllables in these examples:

(1) La flamme éternelle   (2) Une force virile à ta grâce est unie;
    Semble, sur son aile,   Tes couleurs sont une harmonie;
    La pourpre des rois.   Et dans ton enfance un génie
                                   Mit une flamme sur ton front.

(3) Voyez devant les murs de ce noir monastère
    La lune se voiler, comme pour un mystère!

(4) Les humides tapis de mousse   (5) Une colombe descend
    Verdissent tes pieds de satin.   En passant
                                       Blanche sur le luth d'ébène.

(6) Comme si, secouant ses invisibles ailes,
        Un ange passait près de nous.

(7) Venez, Rome à vos yeux va brûler, - Rome entière!

(8) Londres fume et crie. O quelle ville de la Bible!
    Le gaz flambe et nage et les enseignes sont vermeilles

(9) Au calme clair de lune triste et beau,
    Qui fait rêver les oiseaux dans les arbres...

(1) La/flam/me é/ter/nelle   5
     Sem/ble,/sur/son/aile,   5
     La/pour/pre/des/rois.   5

(2) U/ne/for/ce/vi/ri/le à/ta/grâ/ce est/u/nie;   12
     Tes/cou/leurs/sont/u/ne har/mo/nie;   8
     Et/dans/ton/en/fan/ce un/gé/nie   8
     Mit/u/ne/flam/me/sur/ton/front.   8

(3) Vo/yez/de/vant/les/murs/de/ce/noir/mo/nas/tère   12
     La/lu/ne/se/voi/ler,/com/me/pour/un/mys/tère!   12

(4) Le/s hu/mi/des/ta/pis/de/mousse   8
     Ver/dis/sent/tes/pieds/de/sa/tin.   8

(5) U/ne/co/lom/be/des/cend   7
     En/pas/sant   3
     Blan/che/sur/le/luth/d'é/bène.   7

(6) Com/me/si,/se/cou/ant/ses/in/vi/si/ble/s ailes,   12
     Un/an/ge/pas/sait/près/de/nous.   8

(7) Ve/nez,/Ro/me à/vo/s yeux/va/brû/ler, -/ Ro/me en/tière!   12

(8) Lon/dres/fu/me et/crie./O/quel/le/vil/le/de/la/Bible!   13
     Le/gaz/flam/be et/na/ge et/les/en/sei/gnes/sont/ver/meilles   13

(9) Au/cal/me/clair/de/lu/ne/tris/te et/beau,   10
     Qui/fait/rê/ver/les/oi/seaux/dans/le/s arbres...   10

THE ALEXANDRINE

     As you can see, there is a wide variety in the length of line,
but historically, although shorter lines can be lighter (especially if
they have an uneven number of syllables), most French poets have
preferred lines of eight, ten or twelve syllables (the thirteen-
syllable line is very unusual). The most popular of all, the twelve-
syllable line known as the alexandrine, is the French poetic line par
excellence. Various reasons have been put forward for its predominance
- it is convenient for breathing; it is as long as can comfortably be
retained as a sense unit; it easily divides into two balanced halves;
it allows full development of a single feeling or idea; but
especially, it offers the greatest number of possible variations of
rhythm.

     In the so-called Classical alexandrine, the most commonly found
form, the twelve syllables are divided in half by a natural pause or
CAESURA, which is sometimes, though not always, underlined by the
punctuation:

     Dans le coeur des humains les rois ne peuvent lire

So the standard metre for each twelve-syllable line is: six syllables, pause, six syllables, longer pause. But within this metrical framework, the writer can choose his rhythm to suit the content.

Rhythm comes, in any language, from the pattern of stressed and unstressed syllables. In French, stress nearly always falls on the final syllable of a word (aimer, possibilité, regardait), or the last but one if the last syllable is a mute "-e" (parabole, traîtresse). In a phrase, the most significant stress falls on the most significant words - especially verbs and nouns - and on the last syllable before a pause. The poet's choice of where each pause ("coupe" in French) will fall has a significant impact on the rhythm. The Classical alexandrine normally has four stresses, but read these lines aloud, stressing the syllables underlined, to get a feeling of some different patterns:

Dans la nuit des forfaits, dans l'éclat des victoires...

C'est Dieu qui l'a donné, le Dieu de leur prière.

Loin de leur temple en deuil et de leur chaume en cendre.

Reste, ô jeune étranger! reste, et je serai belle.

Je le servirais mieux, si je l'eusse aimé moins.

In these cases, the two HEMISTICHES, or halves of the line, are stressed in the same way. But for the last 150 years poets have been refusing to observe the automatic caesura of the Classical alexandrine, and thus opening up the possibility of a huge range of rhythmic divisions. A common one, for instance, divides the line into three, with stresses on the fourth, eighth and twelfth syllables:

Je suis banni! je suis proscrit! je suis funeste!

It is vital to learn the distinction between metre or syllable count on the one hand, and rhythm or pattern of stress on the other. Perhaps the best book on this is Broome and Chesters, The Appreciation of Modern French Poetry (Cambridge University Press, 1976): the very good introduction has a section on metre and rhythm (pp.7-15), and the book contains several sample commentaries on poems.

With regard to alexandrines, there is a technical term for suppression of the pause at the end of the line: "ENJAMBEMENT" lets the rhythm and the sense run on unbroken into the next line. A famous example comes from Rimbaud's Le Dormeur du Val where the flow of lines 1 to 3, thanks to "enjambement", echoes the flow of the river:

C'est un trou de verdure où chante une rivière
Accrochant follement aux herbes des haillons
D'argent; où le soleil, de la montagne fière,
Luit: c'est un petit val qui mousse de rayons.

Un soldat jeune, bouche ouverte, tête nue,
Et la nuque baignant dans le frais cresson bleu,
Dort; il est étendu dans l'herbe, sous la nue,
Pâle dans son lit vert où la lumière pleut.

Les pieds dans les glaïeuls, il dort. Souriant comme
Sourirait un enfant malade, il fait un somme:
Nature, berce-le chaudement: il a froid.

Les parfums ne font pas frissonner sa narine;
Il dort dans le soleil, la main sur sa poitrine
Tranquille. Il a deux trous rouges au côté droit.

The end of the "enjambement", the isolated word or phrase at the
beginning of the next line ("D'argent" 1.3, "Tranquille" 1.14) is
known as the "REJET" (though this term is occasionally but confusingly
used as a synonym for "enjambement"). Each is emphasised by the stress
falling before a "coupe", and by its isolation: by its sense each
belongs to the previous line, but is cut off by its position; while by
its position each belongs to its own line, but is cut off by its sense
and by the punctuation.

Effects such as "enjambement" or suppression of the caesura are
normally used only sparingly, since they only stand out if the
remainder of the poem is in Classical alexandrines. If there were
"enjambement" at the end of every line, its effect would be lost.

RHYME

As with rhythm, there is a formal aspect to rhyme, and a freer
interpretation of it; let us look at the formal side first.

To describe the RHYME SCHEME of a poem, we conventionally use a
series of small letters, beginning with a. Each rhyming sound gets a
code letter, giving for the Rimbaud lines the rhyme scheme "abab cdcd
eef ggf".

The three most common rhyme schemes have names:

aabbccdd (rhyming couplets)   rimes plates
ababcdcd   rimes croisées
abba cddc   rimes embrassées

You will come to recognise certain FIXED FORMS, such as the sonnet,
ballade or rondeau, which follow a regular pattern of line length,
stanza pattern and rhyme scheme. Some are associated with historical
periods, as also are poetic GENRES such as epigrams (short and pithy),
elegies (longer, more melancholy, often on love or death), and odes
(several regular stanzas on a lofty subject), or broader categories,
including heroic, epic, satirical or lyrical verse.

QUALITY OF RHYME

A definition of rhyme in French poetry would go back to the twelfth and thirteenth centuries. It was then that writers became dissatisfied with mere assonance, in which, in successive lines of verse, only the vowel sound was the same in the final syllable of each line. Thus, in the _Chanson de Roland_ (twelfth century), lines ending in "Charles", "messages", "marche" and "halte" have only the "-a-" sound in common.

With true rhyme, _every_ sound of the final syllable of successive lines of verse is the same.

Nonetheless, it is possible to talk of the quality of different rhymes, with most French critics distinguishing three: "rime pauvre" or "insuffisante", "rime suffisante", and "rime riche".

"Rimes pauvres" have a single rhyming sound: the final stressed vowel, as in peu/feu, vue/remue, disant/lent. Most poets would wish to avoid these.

The most common rhyme is the "rime suffisante", in which there are two rhyming elements, either consonant + vowel (bleuté/comté, bandit/édit - unsounded final consonants do not count) or vowel + sounded consonant (verre/serre, part/fard) or occasionally two successive vowels (océan/mécréant, inouï/réjoui).

Not all critics agree on the definition of "rime riche": for some it is enough that the consonantal group introducing the final stressed vowel is the same in each case (fléchit/enrichit), but a safer rule is to look for at least _three_ identical sounds:

consonant-vowel-consonant:	père/vipère
consonant-consonant-vowel:	heurté/porté
vowel-consonant-consonant:	parte/carte
vowel-consonant-vowel:	quantité/facilité, tondu/fondu

Two successive vowels (see above) may also be counted as "rime riche".

There are limitations on rhymes which have to do with the sense or the derivation of the words used. Rhyme is not totally distinct from sense - indeed, one of its functions is to draw attention to the different meanings of two expressions which sound the same. For this reason, words which have the same meaning or the same root are not acceptable as rhymes (espoir/désespoir, venu/revenu, renoncé/dénoncé). Rhymes which would otherwise be considered rich are not viewed as such if they have a similar nominal, verbal, adjectival or adverbial ending (lecteur/gladiateur, pousseront/glisseront, pacifique/magnifique, lentement/parfaitement), nor if they are so common as to be banal (ombre/sombre, larmes/alarmes). Conversely, a word may rhyme with itself if it is taken in two different senses (e.g. "pas" or "bien" or, in Rimbaud's sonnet, "nue"): this is known as "rime équivoquée". In general, the more dissimilar the words are in meaning, grammatical function and derivation, and the closer they are in sound, the better the rhyme.

One other feature peculiar to French rhyme is the alternation of masculine· and feminine rhymes. A feminine rhyme is one that ends in a mute final syllable ("-e","-es" or "-ent"), a masculine rhyme is anything else. Originally the alternation was to facilitate setting a poem to music, but this purpose has been lost. Nonetheless, most poets keep to the masculine/feminine alternation: in the Rimbaud sonnet, rhymes a, c, e and g are feminine, while b, d and f are masculine.

The French ear is so accustomed to the conventions of poetry, that any departure from them is immediately striking, whether it be "enjambement" or a failure to observe masculine/feminine alternation. Although you will have, initially, to locate mechanically such variations from the norm, you can be certain that they are not accidental: ask yourself what purpose they serve.

Although rhyme has lost the magic effects it may once have been thought to possess, it can still show an incantatory quality, can still make a poem more striking by making it more memorable: it is rhyme that makes verse easier to remember than prose. It also gives harmony and unity to a poem. Repetition of similar rhymes can have a reassuring effect, while very different or unusual ones can be disturbing or amusing. Rhyme brings into correlation two words which sound the same, and a skilful writer can exploit this by leading the reader to link in his mind two words whose meaning is anything but the same, such as "royauté" and "cruauté". And, of course, because it is repeated, the rhyme is one of the most important sounds of a poem.

SOUND

There is no exact correspondence between sound and mood, but sound can certainly help reinforce the mood created by the sense of the words. Read these lines aloud:

Le bruit ébranle l'air, roule, et longtemps encore
Gronde, comme enfermé sous la cloche sonore.
Le silence retombe avec l'ombre... Ecoutez!

In this case, Hugo is describing the midnight bell on a dark night when witches are about. He uses dark, muffled vowels, especially nasals, to evoke the darkness and sinister atmosphere: "ébranle", "roule", "long-", "-temps", "encore", "Gronde", "en-", "sous", "sonore", "-lence", "retombe", "l'ombre". The repeated consonant "r" helps to convey the rolling, lugubrious sound of the bell. Then, to break the mood suddenly, two sharp vowels which catch the attention as much as does the sense of the word: "Ecoutez!"

To feel the impact of the sounds of a poem, it is absolutely essential to read the poem out loud to yourself. Repetition of the same sound (ALLITERATION for consonants, ASSONANCE for vowels) can

reinforce the effect of a single sound, but avoid the temptation to
find alliteration everywhere: it too is an effect to be used
sparingly, and you should find at least three similar sounds and
determine· what mood they imaginatively reflect before claiming that
the author juxtaposed them intentionally. ONOMATOPOEIA is the use of
words formed in imitation of a sound, e.g. "coucou", "miauler". You
will get further help on the connection between sound and sense from
Biard (see p.27) and Broome & Chesters (see p.38).

FREE VERSE

The main characteristic of free verse is that it is without
formal constraints: no fixed rhyme, no fixed length of line or stanza.
The main consequence is that the rhythmic qualities are far more
prominent, as also is assonance. Otherwise, the same poetic resources
are exploited, as in Jacques Prévert's Barbara:

Rappelle-toi Barbara
Il pleuvait sans cesse sur Brest ce jour-là
Et tu marchais souriante
Epanouie ravie ruisselante
Sous la pluie (...)

POETRY COMMENTARY

The section on poetry has been addressed to non-French students
who may have difficulty with Gallic poetic conventions. Consequently,
a good deal of attention has been paid to technical aspects. The
weighting in a verse commentary would be very different, with the
technicalities (line length, rhyme scheme, genre) covered very briefly
towards the beginning, perhaps in as few as four words: "In this
regular sonnet..." The remainder of the commentary would be devoted to
the poet's exploitation of the resources available to him.

Although the emphasis in this manual is on objective rather than
impressionistic criteria, it can be a mistake, especially with poetry,
to try to be too scientific, to explain away every single effect the
poem has had upon you, every nuance of emotion it has evoked. Do not
be mechanical at the expense of intuition.

FURTHER READING

Of the many books dealing with the subtleties and complexities of
French prosody, one of the best known is Maurice Grammont's Petit
traité de versification française (Paris, 10th edition, 1982).

DRAMA

One of the differences between a novel and a poem is the element
of performance. When dealing with a novel, you are confronting the
complete, finished work of art; with a poem, the text itself is
incomplete until it is read aloud, but the reader can perform it
adequately himself.

With drama, the text is no more than a starting point. Reading
aloud is indispensable but insufficient. The script may have within it
the potential to be transformed into a true work of art, but the
resources required - a team of skilled experts and several weeks of
concentrated effort - are not normally at the disposal of the student.
Play texts can seem difficult because of the amount of creative
imagination needed to bring them to life. But simply being aware of
the problem takes you half way to overcoming it.

The other half of the distance between a printed text and a
performance staged in the mind of the reader can be accomplished by
going mentally through the processes that a play normally passes
through before reaching public performance. It is impossible to over-
estimate the benefit derived from actually taking part in a play
production at school or University, either as an actor or back-stage.
You see the hallowed words of Shakespeare or Molière reduced to a dog-
eared script, then gradually brought to life as the comic or dramatic
potential of the script is brought out by the producer and the cast.

To list the stages a text goes through before it truly becomes a
play is also to list the resources that are uniquely available to a
playwright. In terms of conscious choices, the same criteria apply as
to the work of a novelist; but the author of plays must also be aware
that after he has finished, others will make their own conscious
choices in dealing with his text. It is up to him to make things as
easy or as difficult for them as he wishes, to endow his text with a
maximum of potential meaning. He may leave a great deal to the
director, or tie him down to very precise instructions: compare the
extensive and detailed STAGE DIRECTIONS of Victor Hugo with the very
sparse stage directions of the French seventeenth-century tragedians.

One of a director's first concerns is CASTING: should this
character be young or old, tall and svelte or short and fat,
attractive or unattractive? Put yourself in the director's position
and choose players you think are suitable for each part - though be
prepared to change them as you get to know the play better! COSTUME
and MAKE-UP are an extension of casting, since they offer the
possibility of enhancing the characteristics which are to be
communicated visually to the audience. The stage DECOR or SET and the
BACKDROP can also convey a great deal about the characters (compare
the Dallas sets with those for Coronation Street).

In directing individual scenes, you must bear in mind movements
and relative positions on stage (agitated pacing? two characters in
close confrontation? a standing character dominating a sitting

character?), and the stance, gesture and expression of each actor. Will they be hunched dejectedly, walking with a spring in the step, pointing off-stage or shaking an angry fist? Will they be looking into each other's eyes or looking down (shyly? embarrassedly? shamefacedly?) or looking away (indifferently? guiltily? distractedly?). Will the face show pleasure or pain, anger or distress? Does a comic text offer any scope for stage business?

Above all, how will each speech be delivered? What are the qualities of voice to be exploited at any given moment? Will the words be spoken loudly or quietly, and in what tone of voice? Where will the pauses come and what will be the speed of delivery? If you have followed the argument thus far, you will realise that you have now re-encountered, as theatrical director, the same problems you face as a student of commentary: what effect should this script have on the audience, and how can my conscious choices ensure that it _does_ have that effect?

To summarise, then: a theatrical text requires rather different treatment from a piece of prose fiction or a poem. In addition to literary qualities, every aspect of performance must be borne in mind, and the text assessed in terms of what potential is there, and how it might be brought out.

There is a final consideration: the historical evolution of theatrical conventions. The earliest French Classical tragedies, for example, when they were performed at all, were staged in a way quite foreign to modern expectations: not a representational set but merely a row of doorways; no action; no psychological interest; and long speeches, in rhyming couplets, delivered in a formal rather than a naturalistic way, which were no more than stereotyped, rhetorical developments of commonplace themes. The twentieth century theatre with its sophisticated lighting, music and sound effects, its audience participation and its drinks interval is a very different creature, and a history of the theatre would be an essential reference tool for any play commentary. You would also do well to acquire the necessary vocabulary to discuss tragedy (exposition, "noeud", "péripétie", intrigue, catastrophe, "dénouement", catharsis) and comedy (farce, burlesque, vaudeville, "commedia dell'arte", "comédie larmoyante").

And what of cinema and television? They lack the spontaneity of live theatre and the rapport between actors and audience. They may be easier to write about since there is only one performance, fixed for all time, while a play text is always open-ended, and each performance unique. The visual element becomes far more important than in the theatre, to the extent that what was the point of view of the narrator can become the point of view of the camera. Structure depends to a large extent on the editing of the film or videotape. In short, commentary on a film or a television play goes well beyond the scope of this little book.

COMMENTARY ON A SET TEXT

This section should be read as an adjunct to the previous sections on unseen commentary (generalities, structure and style), since these apply equally to commentary on a passage from a set text. The lay-out adopted in this book has meant separating style and content, "forme" and "fond". The intention is to make things clearer for the student, but it must be appreciated that the separation is an artificial one, and that in a good author, style and content are so closely linked as to be inseparable.

You will also notice that more space has been devoted to style than will now be given over to content. This is not because style is more important, or because it will occupy a greater part of your commentary; it is simply because style lends itself more easily to classification. Authors tend to use a common stock of techniques, whereas their content is more individual and less amenable to generalisations. On the other hand, there is sometimes a tendency, when writing on a set text, to concentrate on other issues and neglect detailed analysis of style: this is a temptation to be resisted.

CONTEXT

When you come to tackle commentary on a set text, you will be dealing not with an isolated passage, but with an extract from a book with which you are familiar; so your first task is to place the extract in its context. By context is meant not the chapter and page number, not the entire plot, nothing about the author's life, nothing that does not relate very closely to the extract.

First state the approximate position in the book, for example

"This extract from Gide's L'Immoraliste occurs towards the beginning of the second part, during Michel's stay at La Morinière."

Then say what is happening in the particular sphere or to the particular characters mentioned in the extract, for example

"Marceline is pregnant and Michel, with Charles' help, is getting to know the farm."

Setting the passage in its context should take a maximum of three sentences, and is part of your introduction.

CONTENT

Coverage of links with the rest of the book, on the other hand, should be in the body of the commentary, as part of the detailed analysis. In a literary commentary on a set text, you may find it easier to deal first with the content (its themes and significance for the book as a whole) and then look at stylistic traits; but you will probably find that they overlap so much that it is easier to treat them together, section by section, or, breaking the structure down into minimal units, sentence by sentence.

There are a number of reasons for you to move beyond the passage itself and invoke comparisons with the rest of the book:

- if there is a recurring theme or pattern, ask yourself how the extract fits in or develops it? e.g. Pierre's jealousy in Pierre et Jean, Michel's confusion between the pursuit of pleasure and self-realisation in L'Immoraliste.

- if there is a turning-point or change of direction which affects the rest of the book, e.g. Pierre confronting his mother with his suspicions for the first time (Pierre et Jean).

- if the passage is is significant for what happens later in the book, e.g. Emma's first meeting with Lheureux (Madame Bovary).

- if the extract is particularly significant in the development of one or more characters, e.g. the ball at La Vaubyessard (Madame Bovary).

In every case, the key to a good, relevant commentary is always to take the extract as the point de départ, moving from the extract to the book as a whole, and not trying to drag in extraneous matter (biography, other works, quotations from Euripedes, your own visit last summer to Cabourg, memorable phrases from your tutor's lectures) simply because you hope to impress.

In the conclusion to a commentary on a set text, assess the passage in the context of the work as a whole. Is the content significant, perhaps introducing a new theme or providing the key to a recurring one, or revealing the author's viewpoint, or portraying a character in detail? Are the style and content typical of the work as a whole? Does the passage show those features which characterise the whole work (use of dialogue, or rich, evocative description, or first person narrative, or symbolism, or "style indirect libre", or the historic present, or authorial intervention, or rapid action, or detailed psychological analysis, or extended metaphors, or inconsistent characterisation)? Or does it stand out from the rest of the work by virtue of a distinctive style, for example?

HISTORICAL PERSPECTIVE

At an advanced level, students are often asked to write commentaries on extracts from non-contemporary works. In these cases, an historical appreciation of literary conventions and trends is quite indispensable. To look, for instance, for originality and sincerity in a Ronsard poem or exciting action and naturalistic dialogue in a Corneille tragedy is to risk applying anachronistic criteria.

Literary history is not merely a series of "-isms", but students must know the historical context and trends before tackling a MEDIAEVAL passage (Romance, Chanson de Geste, Courtly Tradition, Fabliau, Dramatic Forms), a SIXTEENTH CENTURY passage (Rhétoriqueur, Humanism, Pléiade, Petrarchism, Neo-Platonism, Reformation), a SEVENTEENTH CENTURY passage (Classicism, Préciosité, Bienséance, Dramatic Conventions, Salon), an EIGHTEENTH CENTURY passage (Enlightenment, Rationalism, Sensibilité, Marivaudage, Revolution), a NINETEENTH CENTURY passage (Romanticism, Realism, Naturalism, Positivism, Le Parnasse, Symbolism) or even a near-contemporary TWENTIETH CENTURY passage (Dada, Surrealism, Existentialism, Nouveau Roman, Theatre of the Absurd).

WRITING A COMMENTARY

HOW TO WRITE A COMMENTARY

Remember that the purpose of a commentary is to help your reader by an analysis of the author's method to see the merits or weakness of the passage under consideration (and, in the case of literary commentary on a set text, the relationship of the extract to the whole work). It cannot be said too often that there is no single correct way of writing a commentary; nonetheless, the following hints should be useful.

1. PREPARATION: COMPREHENSION   Read the passage at least twice to make sure you understand it fully - unnecessary misunderstandings account for a great number of lost marks. Jot down first impressions. Use reference books where necessary. These may include dictionaries, of course, but many other sources of information too. If an author makes his character read a particular book, or go to see a particular opera, or quote a particular verse from the Bible, or refer to a particular classical myth, the choice is not a random one: the reference should convey something of the tastes, knowledge and make-up of the character. If the allusion is unfamiliar to you, you will need to look it up, in a Companion to Literature, a Musical Dictionary, Concordance or a Mythological Dictionary. Atlases and general encyclopedias will also be useful on occasion, and you should get to know where to lay hands on these essential tools.

If individual sentences seem hard to grasp, because of grammatical complexity or elliptical conciseness, struggle with them: they may well turn out to be the most interesting in terms of stylistic commentary.

2. PREPARATION: STRUCTURE   Once you understand the passage, see if the structure divides neatly into sections; if not, can you treat it thematically (e.g. religious aspects, behaviour of character A, behaviour of character B, imagery, dialogue, other stylistic aspects)? It may well be that the best solution will be to divide the passage into its smallest units, in other words adopt a sentence-by-sentence approach. If so, be sure to group related points together, so that

your commentary is not a mere list. In any case, it is vital to plan how you will write the commentary.

3. PREPARATION: NOTES   Make copious brief notes, either section by section or by thematic headings, according to what plan you have settled on. Number the lines, if this has not already been done. Comb the text repeatedly until you have jotted down all the points you think are worth making. Have a look at every single word, though, of course, not every word will be worthy of comment. The check-list on pages 54-5 may well be useful to you at this stage.

4. WRITING THE COMMENTARY: INTRODUCTION   The purpose of the introduction is to help your reader to see the overall trends and themes of the passage, including general characteristics of tone, style, register or narrative point of view. Indicate, in two sentences at most, the content of the passage; also, in the case of commentary on a set text, recall its position in the narrative or play or collection of poems. Indicate which book it is from, with the author's name correctly spelt, and situate the extract in its context. The whole introduction should occupy no more than one or two paragraphs.

5. WRITING THE COMMENTARY: STRUCTURE   Many critics (and generations of French schoolboys) will always begin an "explication de texte" by dividing the passage up into smaller sections, saying where each section begins and ends. This is undoubtedly a useful way to proceed, but only if you can both perceive, and persuade your reader of, what distinguishes one section from the next. Ask yourself if there is a movement from description to narrative, or a balance or contrast between two sections, or a clear progression, or a difference of importance or presentation (e.g. narrative/direct speech), or a change of focus, a transition, a turning point or a climax. How does each section relate to the theme of the passage?

Two words of warning are appropriate here: first, if you end up with numerous sections (say more than five at most), think again; your aim at this point is to show broad movement within the extract, not to paraphrase the entire contents.

Secondly, if you cannot show why you are dividing the passage in a certain way, then it serves no purpose to divide it since it is not a valid way of bringing out the structure. Too many students spend a paragraph explaining where the divisions fall, fail to explain why these divisions have been chosen, and then totally ignore the divisions in the following line-by-line commentary: make sure that you never commit this error.

There are passages which will not lend themselves to division at all. In this case, indicate briefly any salient features of the structure (crescendo, circular structure, etc.) and return to them in the course of your detailed analysis. At most, you may write up to half a page on structure.

6. WRITING THE COMMENTARY: DETAILED ANALYSIS   This is the real meat of the commentary. Remember the golden rules: the aim here is to show what effect is achieved and how it is achieved. Points should be illustrated by quotations from the passage. When dealing with a set text, make sure you link the style and content of the extract with the rest of the book. This part should be fairly straightforward: working from the plan and the copious notes you made earlier, the commentary should more or less write itself.

7. WRITING THE COMMENTARY: CONCLUSION   This is probably the hardest bit. The purpose is to show how the details of style that you have analysed have contributed to the overall effect of the passage. You must bring everything together, link the content and its presentation to show the coherence of the passage.

A brief summary of literary qualities may well help here, but you must beware of mere repetition. The conclusion must be the synthesis that follows the analysis. You are generally advised not to bring in any new points at this stage.

It is in the conclusion of a commentary on a set text that you will assess the extract in the context of the whole work.

PRESENTATION

Presentation is important right from the start: like a shop-window display or the careful presentation of a dish in a restaurant, you can dispose the reader in your favour by writing well, or alienate him by writing badly.

The least impressive, but nonetheless all too frequent, way to begin a commentary is "This passage takes place..." : "this" has not been defined (either for your reader or for your later revision), a passage cannot "take place" (use "occurs" or "is situated" instead), and it is a mechanical and unimaginative opening. A similar phrase ("The passage for commentary is situated...") can provide a safe, if unadventurous, beginning, though you may do better to lead your reader gently into the commentary by starting with a broad statement which can then be linked to the passage. Here are two examples:

Vautrin is normally seen as the most evil character in Balzac's Le Père Goriot, if not in the whole of the Comédie Humaine, but in the passage selected for commentary (pages 102-3) he appears, if not sympathetic, at least as a man capable of warmth in his relations with others.

Camus has so frequently been reproached for the hostility to Arabs which critics find in L'Etranger, that it is valuable to look in detail at the specific passages dealing with the native Oranais. Such is the extract chosen for commentary...

The conclusion, too, should be rounded off; a re-introduction of the broader perspective is more impressive than a bald, abrupt ending.

In the body of the commentary, the presentation is again very important, and you must make every effort to write your commentary in fluent English with correct spelling, correct sentences, correct punctuation and paragraphs. To misspell the names of authors or characters is to wilfully enrage your marker, who will hopefully accept split infinitives and neologisms, but who will be aware that "its" and "it's" are two very different entities and that "hippocracy" is government by horses. Throughout your commentary, vary your expression, so that your work is not boring to read. For instance, instead of repeating the word "emphasise" every time, use "stress", "underline", "focus on", "bring out strongly", "draw attention to", "bring into prominence", "make ... stand out", "throw into relief", etc. Roget's _Thesaurus_ lists synonyms and near-synonyms, is easy to consult, is used by virtually all professional writers, and is available in several cheap paperback editions.

Make your meaning clear, and re-read the final version to make sure it is not _your_ work that is pinned up in the staff room for general amusement. These are three genuine examples of howlers taken from commentaries on Lainé's _La Dentellière_:

> This passage comes near the end of the third part of the book, and so we can assume that it is written by the author (though there is evidence in the passage to suggest otherwise).

> First of all, most noticeable is the appearance of the passage which is broken up into paragraphs. The whole book is the same.

> Pomme says she will sleep with Aimery when he wants. This surprises him as he is old fashioned and wants a nice young virgin to go to bed with.

QUOTATION

The more your work reads like a shopping list, the worse the impression you make, and the lower the mark you get. So you must _not_ simply give quotation - dash - comment, as students sometimes do:

> "Je préfère savoir" - Gertrude is determined to know.

Instead, integrate the quotation into the English sentence, ensuring that your comment is analytical, not merely a translation or paraphrase:

> The conciseness of the statement "Je préfère savoir" stresses the determination and finality of Gertrude's decision.

Make sure that your quotation makes sense as it stands. There are four mistakes especially to be avoided when quoting, the first of which is to leave a quotation that is grammatically unsound. Instead of

> Pierre cannot bear to think of his mother as an adulteress; he wants to "la sût innocente".

write

> Pierre could accept his mother's condemnation by public opinion, "pourvu qu'il la sût innocente, lui, lui seul."

The second mistake is to transcribe, out of laziness, only the opening and closing words of the quotation. If writing it out in full is really going to take an inordinate amount of time, ask yourself whether your point needs illustration at such length.

The third is simply mis-quotation: nothing makes a worse impression than supposed quotations with mis-spellings, missing agreements, and the odd word totally omitted, or a line of poetry that does not scan.

The fourth and most costly is to quote in English and thereby reveal that you have been relying on a translation of the text, rather than the original.

THINGS TO AVOID
(These remarks are based on more than ten years of marking student commentaries.)

IN ANY COMMENTARY

1. Avoid paraphrase and translation: the single most frequent fault in commentary technique. It is assumed that you understand the extract, and that this comprehension will be shown indirectly through accurate analysis, and not directly by your rewriting the passage in your own words. You must always be alert to the danger of simply paraphrasing the content, rather than analysing the author's choice of expression.

2. Avoid writing a series of disjointed remarks: link the points together, and move smoothly from one to the next. If you have said at the beginning that the passage is dramatic or that it reveals a character's weakness, mention how each individual point contributes to the overall drama or the overall character portrayal.

3. Avoid repetition (a particular problem in line-by-line analysis). Again the solution is to group points together, as in the suggested answers to the exercises which follow.

4. Do not wander off the subject: always start from the text. It may sometimes be illuminating to make a brief reference to other fields of

literature (e.g. Camus' debt to the American novel, Petrarchism in Shakespeare's sonnets), but keep it short and relevant.

5. Never say what without saying why, and never make judgments of quality without adducing evidence (usually in the form of a quotation). If you simply state "this is a metaphor", or "he uses short sentences", or "this is effective", or "this is a really good sentence" you will not gain marks for observation, you will lose them for incompetence.

6. Avoid value judgments: a personal response to the text is justified, but beware of introducing your own religious, political or moral prejudices. Assess your subject's skill as an author, not the validity of his views. If the sexism of the illustration that opened the section on imagery (p.20) annoyed you to the extent that you almost failed to grasp the point being made, be warned!

7. In concluding a commentary, do not indulge in exaggerated praise. To state that "Camus is undoubtedly the greatest author the world has ever seen" will probably not impress: stick to what you have managed to prove.

IN COMMENTARY ON A SET TEXT

1. Avoid giving too much detail when situating the passage in context.

2. Avoid character study beyond what is actually alluded to in the extract.

3. Avoid story-telling: whoever reads your commentary will be as familiar with the book as you are, if not more so. It is assumed that you know the whole story: prove it by intelligent and selective allusion, not by retelling the whole thing in your own words.

4. As always, avoid paraphrase and translation.

FURTHER READING

There has not been space here to consider the different schools of literary criticism, or different approaches to literary commentary. Once you have assimilated the basics, look at other books on the subject in your library. Some, you may find, are written from a great height, and assume an acquaintance with literature and a command of literary analysis which are quite unrealistic. However, Advice to the Student of French, by R.C. Knight and F.W.A. George (Oxford, Basil Blackwell, 3rd edition, 1973), although dated in many respects, is still well worth reading, especially the section on commentary, pp.51-61, and the examples pp.93-103. And as a next step in furthering your skills, I recommend W.D. Howarth and C.L. Walton, Explications: The Technique of French Literary Appreciation (Oxford University Press, 1971), which has an excellent introduction, several model commentaries, and a thorough bibliography which will suggest further

reading for you. Also to be recommended are W.M. Frohock's French
Literature: An Approach Through Close Reading (Cambridge, Mass., 1964)
and H. Bénac's Vocabulaire de la dissertation (Hachette, 1949), which
is now nearly forty years old, but still of use to those writing
commentaries or essays in French.

Many collections of model commentaries have been published,
illustrating the kind of thing students might write if only they too
were professors with twenty years' experience behind them. You may
find these useful if you regard them as a beginner at tennis might
view a Wimbledon final: learn from others, imitate their strong
points, but do not be discouraged by their consummate skill, nor hope
to equal them just yet.

CONCLUSION

It is increasingly alleged that society is moving into a post-
literary (or even post-literate!) phase. If true, this is a great
pity, for the written heritage of all cultures is a treasure-house
from which the intelligent and imaginative reader can derive limitless
benefit and pleasure. No other medium can ever reproduce the magic
which results from combining the author's creative imagination and
skill with the reader's imaginative response.

A basic training manual like this one may unintentionally give
the impression that an analytical approach to literature is a
mechanical and joyless exercise. This should never be the case, since
literary commentary is an exercise to enhance your reading technique,
and literature is an area of human activity, like golf or love-making,
in which the pleasure increases as the technique improves.

SUMMARY AND CHECK-LIST

(ST = Commentary on a set text, P = Poetry)

1. Read and Understand.

2. Full notes of points to be made.

3. Arrange notes into plan, to which you refer at each succeeding stage.

4. Short introduction:
   ST Situate passage (one or two sentences).
   Content: summarise very briefly.
   Nature of passage: narrative, description, atmosphere, background, reflection, analysis, dialogue, indirect speech, etc.
   Tone: comic, tense, emotional, tragic, satirical, lyrical, etc.
   Register: slang, oratorical, journalistic, etc.
   Point of view: first or third person.

5. Structure:
   Divisions and what distinguishes them.
   Movement, focus, development, climax, circular structure, etc.

6. Detailed commentary: EFFECT ACHIEVED - HOW - SUPPORTING QUOTATION.
   N.B. This list follows the structure of earlier sections of the book; it does NOT reflect either the relative importance of each item or the order in which they should be presented.
   Imagery: simile, metaphor (extended, dead or mixed), abstract or concrete, personification, analogy, allegory, myth, symbolism; visual, emotional, intellectual, underlining a quality; original, striking, appropriate.
   Sentence structure: complex, simple; short, long sentences; ellipsis; rhythm, balance, harmony, emphasis in word order.
   Rhetorical devices: exclamations, rhetorical questions, anacolutha, anaphora, antiphrasis, apostrophe, chiasmus, hyperbole, litotes, metonymy, oxymoron, periphrasis, synecdoche, zeugma.
   Vocabulary: precise, vague, ambiguous, enigmatic, banal, evocative, rich in association, figurative, sensual, emotive, exotic, erotic, religious, mystical, hyperbolic, understated, superlative, negative, ironic, idiomatic, abstract, concrete, onomatopoeic, technical, archaic, pedantic, didactic, humorous, comic, incongruous; pun, cliché, neologism, circumlocution; verb tenses and frequency; adjectives (for the intellect, emotions, senses - which senses?); colour, expressiveness; juxtaposition, contrast, paradox, repetition, gradation, enumeration, accumulation.
   Sound and rhythm.
   P Rhyme and versification.
   ST Links of theme, character, style with the rest of the book (may be half or more of the whole commentary).
   AVOID paraphrase, story-telling, irrelevance, careless English.

7. Conclusion:
   ST Extract in relation to the whole work: how important, how
   typical in style and content.
   (Summary and) synthesis of previous points.
   Judgment of passage's overall quality and unity.
   AVOID mere repetition.

EXERCISE

Write comprehensive notes for a commentary on

(i) the extract from Maupassant's *Pierre et Jean* (p.18 above) in which the doctor visits different parts of the liner "Lorraine", bound for New York;

(ii) Rimbaud's *Le Dormeur du Val* (pp.38-9 above).

When you are wholly satisfied that your notes are complete (use the check-list on pp.54-5), compare your answer with the notes below. Bear in mind that there is no single correct answer to a commentary, and do not be dismayed if the lay-out, the details and the conclusion of your commentary are very different from what follows.

(i) Maupassant: *Pierre et Jean.*
Theme: contrast between rich and poor passengers on board ship - only the two extremes are described, to heighten the contrast.
Structure: first and third paragraphs frame the more important central section; paragraph 1 sets the scene, telling us of Pierre (awake), time of day (morning), situation (boat-train unloading passengers on to the "Lorraine"); in paragraph 2, we look through Pierre's eyes at what follows - "il erra" line 4, "il entra" 8, "descendit" 21, "pénétrant" 22, like roving eye camera. Rich first-class passengers 9-18 (climax "millionnaires") contrasted with emigrants 20-33 (climax near-starvation); paragraph 3 gives Pierre's reaction, with which the reader is associated.

Activity suggested in paragraph 1 ("mouvements des matelots" 1, imperfect "arrivait" 3) expanded in 4-7, with added anxiety common to all departures, reinforced by present participles and broken rhythm of enumeration ("affairés" 4, "inquiets", "cherchant", "s'appelant" 5, "se questionnant" 5-6, "se répondant", "effarement" 6). Noise and incoherence in last three participles and "au hasard" 6.

Brief narrative 7-8 brings focus back to doctor.

Descriptive elements of first-class accommodation:
Cosmopolitan: "Anglais" 9, "cosmopolite" 14, "tous les continents" 15.
Places alluded to ("salon" 9, "Anglais" evokes gentleman's club 9, "hall flottant" 14, "grands hôtels", "théâtres" 16, "lieux publics" 17) suggest status and luxury and that, with cosmopolitanism, the rich ("riches" 15, "millionnaires" 18) are at home anywhere.
Uncrowded: "quelques" 9.
Spaciousness ("dans les coins" 9-10, "grande pièce" 10, "prolongeait indéfiniment... perspective" 11-12, "longues tables... lignes illimitées" 12-13, "vaste" 14, unbroken length of sentence 10-13) associated with brilliance, opulence of luxury fittings and furniture ("marbre blanc" 10, "filets d'or", "glaces" 11, "longues tables" 12, "sièges tournants", "velours grenat" 13, "luxe opulent" 16, "luxe imposant" 17).
Ease, idleness, no real worry: "sommeillaient" 9, "satisfait" 17.
Life in first-class seems desirable, but full of objects not people: emptiness and soullessness stress superfluity; Maupassant's disapproval reflected in bad taste of it all: "imposant et banal" 17.

Transition 18-20 skips over intermediate group, sharpens contrast.

Descriptive elements of steerage passengers

Contrast at once between those who act and those who are acted upon:
Rich are active and vocal, subject of several verbs; poor are the
object of an impersonal verb - "on avait embarqué" 20 - without voice
or will-power.
Portrayed at once as animals- "troupeau" 21 - then as beneath animals
in comparison 23-24; only active verb ("grouillant" 27) reinforces
dehumanisation.
Rich are distinguishable individuals (verbs 5-6, "quelques" 9), poor
are indivisible mass, have lost individuality: "troupeau" 21,
"humanité" 22, "chair" 23, "centaines d'hommes, de femmes et
d'enfants" 26-7, "tas", "ne distinguait point" 28, "foule" 29 & 30.
Rich had space for few, poor are many in a cramped area: "planches
superposées" 27, "souterrain obscur et bas" 25, simile "pareil aux
galeries des mines" 25-6; last two emphasise claustrophobia as well as
darkness, echoed in "ne distinguait point" 28 and "voyait vaguement"
29, contrast to lightness and opulent colour above ("blanc", "d'or",
"glaces", "grenat").
Metaphor linked rich accommodation to hotels and theatre, suggesting
light, leisure, comfort; equivalent simile of mine defines the exactly
opposite lot of the poor: darkness, work, discomfort.
Rich have a palatial room just for eating (they have cabins 5): poor
eat and sleep in one small space.
No wonder first picture is essentially visual, second characterised by
smell (reflecting cramped space, too dark to see anyway).
Luxury above contrasts with sordidness, dirt and smell ("odeur" 22,
"mal propre", "puanteur", "nue" 23, "sordide", "haillons" 29),
associated with poverty ("pauvre" 23, "misérables" 30) and total lack
of any refinements: just "planches" 27 and "sol" 28. Strength of
observer's reaction ("saisi" 22) in synonymous adjectives expressing
physical disgust: "nauséabonde" 22, "écoeurante" 23.
Pathos of presence of women and children (26-7) increased by
adjectives underlining the effects of poverty: "femme maigre",
"enfants exténués" 31.
Passivity of poor again stressed by similar-sounding past participles:
"étendus" 27, "vaincus", "épuisés", "écrasés" 30, "exténués" 31; they
are victims, acting not out of choice (new land is "inconnue" 32) but
necessity. Only verb with poor as subject is "espéraient" (32), which
is ironic when we see how low and negative their hopes are (starvation
32-3 contrasted with dinner setting 12-13) and that even these may not
be realised: "peut-être" 33 in unusual and heavily stressed position.

Paragraph 3, omniscient narrator takes us into Pierre's thoughts;
having seen with his eyes we are likely to share his reflexions.
Activity in 34-6 ("travail" twice, "efforts", "lutte acharnée",
"énergie") takes us beyond immediate situation on boat to desperate
conditions of life for the working poor - harsh but positive. But each
noun inexorably negated by adjective ("perdu", "stériles", "vain",
"dépensée") and by what we have already seen. By holding back "par ces
gueux" (36), Maupassant allows previous two lines to have universal
validity.
Enumeration of 34-6 suggested repeated failure, echoed in "re-" (35 &
36) and "encore" (37), as "sans savoir où" (37) echoes "inconnue"
(32): the rich at home anywhere, the poor nowhere. End of balanced
contrast of details between rich and poor.

Direct speech in 38-9 dramatic, even though never pronounced. Effect on doctor shown by "crier" 38, vulgarity of "foutez-vous" 38, use of vocabulary suited to animals ("femelles", "petits" 39), inability to remain with them. Reader invited to share his "pitié" (40) as the scene changes ("s'en alla"), but no need to draw explicit moral: contrast itself is eloquent.

If the passage were from a set text, you should begin your commentary by placing it in context.
Context: Very near the end of Guy de Maupassant's _Pierre_ et _Jean_ (1888); on Jean's initiative, Pierre is leaving his family, feeling lonely and depressed, trying to put jealousy and vengeance behind him. He is a suitable narrator, since he too is exploring the boat for the first time.
You could also add, concerning paragraph 3: Rich/poor contrast inevitably recalls, in a grotesquely distorted way, his own situation and resentment. Lines 34-6 seem, in his self-pity, to apply to him as much as the emigrants; his own despair partially explains the strong emotion behind the exhortation to suicide, his need to flee them; Maupassant's "pitié" is thus ironic: Pierre's feelings not all altruistic.

(ii) Rimbaud: _Le Dormeur du Val_.
Theme: picture of dead young man contrasted with idyllic natural setting, suggesting man's defilement of nature by war. Conflict between peace of nature and violence of man not new (cf Hugo's _La Nature_).
Versification: sonnet, alexandrines, rhyming abab cdcd eef ggf with masculine/feminine alternation.
Background: written 1870, Rimbaud only 16; France at war with Germany, may reflect a personal experience; R later abandoned literary career, wanted this poem destroyed.
Structure: Title and early lines paint peaceful picture, man initially introduced apparently in harmony with setting, asleep. Gradual disquiet builds to final confirmation that he is dead.
Title: "Dormeur" + "Val": two key-words introduce recurring themes: sleep and nature.
Sleep suggests warmth, comfort, calm, security, contentment, is recalled in nearly every line: "Dort" in line 7, "son lit" 8, "dort" 9, "somme" 10, "berce-le" 11, "dort" 13. This gives overall tone and unity to poem, but becomes increasingly unreal.
Nature evoked largely by suggestion, not statement, cf synaesthesia (fusion of the senses) of _Correspondances_ of Baudelaire (admired by R). Main feature is colour, directly portrayed ("argent" 3, "bleu" 6, "verdure" 7, "vert" 8) or impressionistically suggested ("herbes" 2, "herbe" 7, "nue" 7, "glaïeuls" 9). Second feature movement, but as in idyll, all is still except river and light playing on it. Movement suggested by picturesque metaphors: "accrochant follement" 2, "mousse de rayons" 4 visual evocation of light on moving water, with "follement" and "mousse" (cf champagne) suggesting happy celebration. "chante" 1 adds sound of movement, word chosen for pleasant connotations, as is "parfum" 12: satisfaction of all the senses.
Many contrasts, two of them contributing to idyllic setting: intimacy of "petit val" 4/majestic setting of personified "montagne fière" 3; bright sunlight ("soleil" 13, "lumière pleut" image 8, sparkling on water) and coolness ("frais cresson" 6, moving water 1-4). Link

between sunlight and water in both "mousse de rayons" which ends first quatrain and "lumière pleut" which ends second quatrain - symmetry. Major opposition is between the idyllic scene and death, but at first reading the clash is not evident: careful structure misleads the reader/listener to misinterpret. Thus the idyllic setting of first quatrain conditions us to see only certain connotations of "soldat" 5: not violence and bloodshed but perhaps brightly-coloured uniform. This impression confirmed by "jeune" (stressed by inverted word order), by his being alone, by the fact he is not fighting; relaxation and sleep perhaps deeper after exertion, and "bouche ouverte", "tête nue" (no protective helmet) stress the vulnerability which comes not from danger but from a feeling of total security (protection of mother nature). "nuque baignant" 6 and "étendu" 7 suggest total abandonment, relaxation, voluntary but born of exhaustion: impression confirmed by "pâle" 8; youth, tiredness, vulnerability evoke reader's sympathy. Disquiet perhaps aroused by "pieds dans les glaïeuls" 9 (uncontrolled abandonment?) but calmed by repetition of "sourire" 9 & 10, recalling warmth and welcome of nature in first quatrain. "enfant" 10 recalls vulnerability of youth, thus outweighs the unsettling "malade" 10, which is put down to fatigue.

Line 12 is the first inescapable evidence of something wrong, because of contrast between man (cold) and surroundings (warm); apostrophe to Nature as protector and mother-figure ("berce" 12) increases concern, reader's subconscious disquiet becomes a consciously perceived contradiction. In this light, all that preceded is re-interpreted: "soldat" resumes connotations of war, unprotected head and open mouth, uncontrolled sprawl half in the river become sinister. Nonetheless, subtle tension between hope that all is well (created by title and early lines) and fear of death is maintained till the very end, by continuing references to pleasant things ("parfums" 12) and by ambiguity of "Tranquille" 14.

Last sentence litotes: calm and prosaic tone emphasise horror, exactitude of number and position = unemotional narration, evokes emotion in reader.

In many ways, as suggested throughout poem, soldier is in harmony with suroundings: motionless, secure, resting; but underlying antithesis life/death, beauty/horror brought out especially by colour: "rouges" 14 clashes with gentle green, blue and silver, darkness with lightness.

Simplicity of lexis makes poem very direct: all vocabulary commonplace, including some (army) slang: "trou de verdure" 1, "somme" 10. But impressionism in vocabulary of first quatrain: in 1-3, only "herbes" has its literal meaning, but consistent picture of swift-moving water obstructed by weed or overhanging grass, and thus creating irregularly-shaped patterns of reflected light. "lumière pleut" 8 (only other image in poem except bed/sleep) more conventional, but ties water and sun together.

Simplicity of sentence construction: only four subordinate clauses altogether, but carefully structured. First quatrain: "c'est un" main clause + "où" clause + "où" clause + "c'est un" main clause. First tercet: long phrase + short main clause with "il" subject, three times. All this balanced repetition adds to aura of calm and order. Rhythmical exploitation of alexandrine: through enjambement 2-3 and suppression of caesura 2 unrestrained flow of water; rejet "D'argent" stresses sunlight; "luit" 4 in similar stressed position for same effect; likewise "Dort" 7 - verb suspended to end of sentence in both cases. Sometimes natural, conversational speech rhythm (1, 4);

sometimes grammatical structure overruns lines (9-10); triadic rhythm
of enumeration in 5 followed by uninterrupted flow of 6 and internal
rhyme of 7 reinforces harmony. Positioning of "Tranquille" after
enjambement further enhances the ambiguity: what is "tranquille"? -
the scene, "Il", "main" or "poitrine"? The first three mean peace and
harmony, the fourth death, but separation of noun and adjective
maintain suspense as long as possible. Long pause and series of
precise monosyllables in the final line leave no doubt.